MW01124432

West *of*
Paradise

West *of* Paradise

Exploring SOUTHEASTERN ARIZONA

Carolyn Niethammer

RIO NUEVO PUBLISHERS
Tucson, Arizona

For my brother Tom. As kids we learned to love Arizona's byways from the back seat of our parents' Jeep.

Acknowledgments

I AM GRATEFUL TO ALL THOSE WHO GAVE THEIR TIME AND EXPERTISE to help me tell this story. The ever-generous Jeanne Williams offered a bed, introductions, and great information based on her long residence in Southeastern Arizona. Dorothy Burkhart provided a home away from home. Ford Burkhart and Barbara Chinworth were cheerful traveling companions. Jay Quade, director of the Desert Lab, explained the dramatic history of Arizona geology. Also helpful were Mima Falk, Shel Clark, Fran Zweifel, John R. Ratje, Ed Sawyer, Linda Brewer, Christine Conte, and Nancy Roush. Tom Sheridan's *Arizona: A History* was a tremendous resource. Gail Hartmann, Roy Johnson, and Ford Burkhart read sections of the book and gave good advice.

RIO NUEVO PUBLISHERS
An imprint of Treasure Chest Books
P.O. Box 5250, Tucson, Arizona 85703-0250
(520) 623-9558, www.rionuevo.com

© 2003 by Carolyn Niethammer
All rights reserved.

No part of this book may be reproduced, stored, or introduced into a retrieval system, or otherwise copied in any form without the prior written permission of the publisher, except for brief quotations in reviews or citations.

Editors: Ronald J. Foreman and James Reel

Design: Larry Lindahl, Lindahl-Bryant Studio

Map: Andy Mosier, reprinted with permission
of Madden Publishing

Library of Congress Cataloging-in-Publication Data

Niethammer, Carolyn J.
  West of Paradise : exploring Southeastern Arizona /
Carolyn Niethammer.
    p. cm.
  ISBN 1-887896-57-6 (pbk. : alk. paper)
  1. Arizona—Guidebooks. I. Title.
  F809.3.N54 2003
  917.91 50454—dc21
                                    2003005770

Printed in Korea

10 9 8 7 6 5 4 3 2 1

CONTENTS

Old West
New West

1. SOUTHEASTERN ARIZONA was the stage for the great American drama that we call the Old West. This is where Geronimo, Johnny Ringo, and Wyatt Earp played out the lives that have been retold in countless movies and Western novels. Here you'll find Spanish missions and vast ranches with rolling grasslands. You can stroll on boardwalks where the Tombstone gunfighters fought and explore Apache Spring near the ruins of Fort Bowie.

In a canyon of the Chiricahua Mountains, you'll even find Paradise. Located almost on the New Mexico border, Paradise was once a thriving town with a hotel and several saloons. Virtually abandoned for decades, it is now home to a handful of folks who have shooed out the lizards and spiders and restored some of the old buildings.

But Southeastern Arizona is more than its romantic past. It also houses atop Mount Graham a collection of the most powerful telescopes in the world. On the plain below, vineyards produce award-winning Cabernets and Merlots. An industry has grown up to welcome tourists who come for outdoor activities

A rock climber in Dry Canyon looks out toward Sierra Vista and the Whetstone Mountains. ANDREW KORNYLAK

or to just relax and soak up the sun. Bird-watchers seek out more than 400 species that live in or visit the area. And throughout the region, ranchers, environmentalists, and government agencies have banded together to use the latest scientific research to ensure that the beauty of the land will endure for generations.

For most visitors, the gateway to this fascinating and picturesque region is Tucson, a sophisticated metropolitan university town. While Tucson boasts many cosmopolitan attractions, it is outside the city—in the small towns and rural areas—where the coyotes still yip at sunset and you can stand under a deep blue canopy of sky stretching from horizon to horizon and not see another sign of human habitation. This book concentrates on the far southeastern corner of Arizona that extends from US Interstate 19 (also called the Nogales Highway) to the border of New Mexico, and from slightly north of US Interstate 10 south to the international border with Mexico. This diverse area of deserts, mountains, and canyons encompasses parts of Pima, Santa Cruz, and Graham Counties and all of Cochise County.

Birth of a Landscape

The topography of Southeastern Arizona looks like that of few other places on earth. Long, narrow mountain ranges run north to south and are separated by broad valleys. Wherever you stand in those valleys, you can see a mountain range to the east and west, and sometimes to the north and south as well. The lowest valleys are about 3,000 feet in elevation and the highest mountains more than 10,000 feet—over a mile in vertical change. Geologists refer to this kind of landscape as basin-and-range terrain.

How did the land get to be this way? When geologists explain the process, they consider periods of time that are inconceivable to most nonscientists. We could start the story 250 million years ago, when a shallow ocean covered much of Arizona. That was when the Dos Cabezas and Whetstone Mountains, all ocean sediment, were laid down. Today they are rich with marine fossils such as trilobites, shark and fish teeth, and corals that testify to their earlier status as tropical reefs.

Skip ahead 100 million years to the Jurassic period, when rumbling volcanoes dotted the landscape of Arizona. The magma that was not expelled from the deep chambers of these glowing caldrons cooled and became granite. Over the next 20 million years, the exterior of the volcanoes eroded away. Along Interstate 10, we can see what was deep inside those volcanic plumbing systems in the granite that forms the boulders in Texas Canyon, just north of Dragoon. The weathering over the millions of years has rounded and smoothed the rock into its present shapes. Move forward in time another 100 million years or so to 30 million years ago. More volcanic activity. Just to the south of what are now the Chiricahua Mountains, glowing avalanches blew out of the volcanoes. The eruptions went on for about 5 million years, with lava and ash forming a layer of rock known as rhyolite tuff almost one-third of a mile deep.

When things quieted down somewhat, the rock began to cool, and the inevitable process of erosion took over again. At the same time—that would be about 25 million years ago—the tectonic plates on which the earth's crust sits began to move and the fluid crust below the surface began to stretch from east to west, cracking into long narrow sections that were uplifted and became the mountain ranges. The lower areas between the mountains dropped further and formed valleys.

Bull Field, oil painting by Alysa Bennett of the 99 Bar Ranch, Douglas.

Sycamore trees with Cathedral Rock in the background, seen from Cave Creek Canyon in the Chiricahua Mountains. LARRY ULRICH

That brings us to 6 million years ago, which is fairly recent in geologic time. As more ice ages came and went and came again, the higher portions of the mountains eroded and filled in the valleys with sand, gravel, and clay.

The mountains are still being pulled apart today. Scientists consider any geologic movement within the last hundred years to be "active." Stark evidence that the surface is still moving came from an earthquake just south of Douglas in 1887 that was strong enough to crack walls in Bisbee, throw stagecoach horses to their knees at Fort Bowie, and bend railroad tracks. Mountain peaks, trees and all, were tossed into adjacent canyons. New artesian springs appeared, and others dried up. You may not feel it, but every day the ground in Southeastern Arizona is shifting, continuing the process of building mountains and valleys.

From Mammoths to Railroads

For 13,000 years, people have considered Southeastern Arizona a fine place to live. We have evidence of the existence of very early hunters at Greenbush Draw near Naco, at nearby Lehner Ranch, and at Murray Springs near Sierra Vista. In these spots, all close to the San Pedro River, archaeologists have found fluted stone spear points, animal-butchering tools, and remnants of fires among the bones of 11 different mammals, including early tapirs, bison, and mammoths. The mammoths were much larger than today's elephants, yet these hunters brought them down with nothing but lances with chipped stone points.

At that time Arizona was beginning to enter another stage in its endless cyclical climate change and was becoming much drier and warmer. By the end of the next thousand years the mammoths were extinct, and the Indians who relied on big game had to adapt to new conditions. It appears that for the next 10,000 years, small nomadic groups moved throughout Southeastern Arizona, subsisting on small animals, nuts, seeds, cactus fruit, and wild greens.

It wasn't until about 1000 B.C. that people settled into more permanent communities, began to grow corn in irrigated fields, and built round, brush-covered homes in shallow pits. Then, beginning around A.D. 1200, still-unexplained changes swept through all the

A traditional Apache wickiup on display along the trail to Fort Bowie. LARRY LINDAHL

Indian cultures in the Southwest. Throughout Southeastern Arizona, people began to build aboveground structures, some with multiple stories, which have become known as pueblos. Many of these communal dwellings were organized around large kivas, or round underground structures used for religious purposes. Remnants of these structures have been found north of Benson and at the entrance to canyons in the Chiricahuas and other mountains. But after only 200 years, the pueblos were abandoned.

Archeologists and anthropologists are still asking why. It appears that people continued to live in Southeastern Arizona, albeit in much smaller numbers, and they lived very simply, leaving few traces for archaeologists to find.

When the Spanish missionaries arrived in 1691 they found farmers living in small villages along the San Pedro and Santa Cruz Rivers. At the same time, Athabaskan people were drifting down from the Great Plains into what would become New Mexico and Arizona. Those who finally made it to Southeastern Arizona became known as the Chiricahua Apache. They captured horses that had escaped from European explorers, learned to ride, and began to take over most of what is known today as Cochise County, an area larger than Connecticut. The Indians hunted and gathered but also became expert at raiding the villages of other Native Americans and capturing cattle from Hispanic and, eventually, Anglo settlers living on ranches.

The Spanish had established missions, *presidios* (forts), and a few ranches along the Santa Cruz and San Pedro Rivers, but the Apaches attacked relentlessly. Most of the Europeans decided the area was indefensible, abandoned the ranches they'd developed on land grants, and returned to Mexico. The Spanish eventually managed to pacify at least some of the Apaches through economic incentives, bribing them with liquor, beef, and sometimes-defective firearms. For a while, life was a little more peaceful for the other Indians in the area as well as for the European settlers.

When Mexico gained independence in 1821, the Spanish garrisons were withdrawn from the frontier

TIPS FOR A TROUBLE-FREE TRIP

WESTERN MOVIES are famous for dramatizing the difficulties of living and traveling in the Old West. Waterholes were miles apart, venomous snakes lurked behind rocks, outlaws hid out at remote ranches, and Indians swooped down without warning. The plants were prickly, and those cloudless blue skies, while beautiful, did nothing to shield you from the piercingly hot sun.

Trail, oil painting by Alysa Bennett of the 99 Bar Ranch, Douglas.

More than a hundred years later, about the only thing that has changed is that we no longer fear Indian attacks. As you travel through Southeastern Arizona, you might see an announcement about a poetry reading by N. Scott Momaday or a flute concert by R. Carlos Nakai, both Native Americans. Or you might find Indians from any of Arizona's tribes fixing computers, selling insurance, pumping your gas, or working on a state highway crew.

But water remains scarce, you should watch out for snakes, it always gets really hot in the summer, and, yes, there are still some bad guys out there.

HERE ARE SOME TIPS TO MAKE YOUR TRIP A SAFE ONE:

1. *If you are planning to hike in the backcountry or drive on unimproved roads, don't go alone.* Decide where you're going to hike or explore and, whether or not you have a companion, let somebody know your plan—the motel owner, the RV park host, a park ranger. Stick to the plan. If you don't return, somebody can go looking for you.

2. *Make sure your vehicle is in good working order; check the spare tire and your jack.* Your cell phone may not work to help you call for assistance, so you'll need to be self-reliant.

3. *Take plenty of water for both yourself and the car.* Keep drinking the water, even if you are not thirsty. Dehydration can be deadly.

territories. The brand-new Mexican republic was poor and couldn't afford to continue to buy off the Apaches, so the Indians started raiding again. Despite that threat, a few more settlers came in with their tough mixed-breed longhorn cows and high hopes of turning the grasslands into prosperous ranches. Then, after too many deaths and too many other losses to the Apaches, they, too, gave up, and by 1840 the big ranches became Apache land again.

After the United States fought Mexico for Texas and California and won, it needed to build a railroad to connect the southern states to California. So in 1854 the United States paid Mexico $10 million for what is now southern Arizona and southern New Mexico as part of the Gadsden Purchase.

Unlike Mexico, the United States had the resources to send military forces to contain the

The current B-Troop, 4th U.S. Cavalry Regiment, was established at Fort Huachuca in 1973 as a memorial unit, representing the U.S. Army's participation in the Indian Wars of the Southwest.

Apaches. With greater security, the Mexican residents decided to reclaim their large ranches, and others moved in. People from other parts of the United States slowly began to settle in the area as well.

4. *Wear a broad-brimmed hat and sunscreen.* University of Arizona doctors urge you to reapply the sunscreen every three hours or so. One morning application isn't sufficient for a whole day of exposure.

5. *If you'll be hiking, pack a knapsack with the following: matches, a sweatshirt or light jacket, a whistle, a signal mirror, Band-Aids, snack bars, an elastic bandage, and a flashlight.* A lightweight Mylar sheet (sometimes called a space blanket) can fold to the size of a postage stamp but will help you conserve body heat if it gets cool or you need to spend the night outdoors.

If you become lost, be extremely careful in lighting a signal fire. Clear the area down to the dirt for a 15-foot radius around the fire and make it a very small one. In one summer alone, hikers in Southern Arizona inadvertently set fires that burned hundreds of thousands of acres of Arizona's dry forests, including many homes, and nearly took the lives of the fire-setters as well as the firefighters.

6. *As you hike, pay attention to where you put your feet and your hands.* Do not reach blindly under or behind a rock — this is where snakes and scorpions

hang out. Should you get bitten, try to remain calm (snake and scorpion bites are rarely deadly). Move away from the snake. Don't cut the skin to try to suck out the venom from a snakebite. If the bite is on your hand or arm, remove rings, bracelets, and watches and keep the bite below your heart. Try to get to your car and drive to a hospital as soon as possible, preferably within an hour. If the delay will be more than a half hour, wrap an elastic bandage between the bite and your trunk about the same tightness as you'd wrap a sprained ankle; don't cut off circulation.

7. *Remember that you can't tell outlaws by black hats, as in the movies.* In this region, there is a constant flow of drug smugglers and illegal entrants from Mexico. Most of these people want to remain inconspicuous, so if you suspect you may have come upon some smugglers while you're in a remote area, just give them a wide berth. Get in your car and drive away. Most migrants are not dangerous, just poor people looking for jobs and a better life, but you have no way of telling who's who.

Play it safe. You can always make the story more elaborate later when you tell it to your friends. Who'll know?

Two Bisbee miners prepare to go down a raise, perhaps in the Copper Queen Mine, circa 1910. The tracks in this haulage tunnel accommodated ore cars pulled by mules.

extension of the plants of northern Mexico's Sierra Madre Occidental. The zone also sits between two deserts, the Chihuahuan Desert to the east and the Sonoran Desert to the west. Plants from all these areas have settled in wherever they can find a comfortable niche or microclimate.

Most plants that grow in Southeastern Arizona have to make some adaptation to heat and drought. Rain showers here are typically quick, penetrating only a short way into the soil. Succulents, such as prickly pear, cholla, and barrel cacti, have shallow root systems that spread far beyond the plant that you see above the ground. In this way they can use whatever rain that falls, gathering the moisture in a circle extending out several feet from their base. These succulents also have waxy, thick skin that allows them to store water efficiently. During a prolonged drought, some plants, such as yuccas and agaves, can actually put their metabolism on idle and wait for rain. Other plants, such as brittlebush and bursage, enter deep dormancy, dropping their leaves and becoming seemingly lifeless sticks until they have access to moisture again.

The Southeastern Arizona grasslands are covered with perennial grasses that can take advantage of shallow rains with their thick mat of roots close to the surface of the soil. When rains arrive during the warm weather of the summer and early fall, it takes only one day for these grasses to send out new roots and begin growing. Then what had been a vista of many shades of gold and buff since the previous summer turns lush green as far as you can see, and wild sunflowers grow six feet tall. When the nights turn chilly in October and the rains stop, the green fades quickly to pale brown again.

In this generally hot, relentlessly sunny region, the riparian areas are the precious jewels of the

The discovery of rich ore in Tombstone and Bisbee in 1878 and the completion of the Southern Pacific Railroad from Tucson to El Paso in 1881 combined with the eventual pacification of the Apaches in 1886 to make the area even more attractive to settlers. Migrants began to flood in, exploiting the area's richness through ranching and mining.

A Niche in a Dry Land

Four different plant communities converge in Southeastern Arizona, making the area unusually rich in vibrant flowers, trees, and other growing things. This region is the southern border of the Rocky Mountain group of plants and the northern ecosystem. A different set of plants flourishes where water flows year-round or, in drier periods, stays not far below the surface. Near the San Pedro River, Sonoita Creek, and Cienega Creek, we find willows and tall, shady cottonwoods with golden leaves that in the fall provide all the autumn foliage many desert dwellers ever get to enjoy.

A prescribed burn near Fort Huachuca.
MILLS TANDY

The effect of people on the natural landscape can't be discounted. In the southwestern United States, only five percent of what were originally riparian areas remain. As the water table is drawn down, these spots become increasingly fragile and only constant vigilance can sustain them.

Interestingly, our love of the land—and even our best efforts to protect it—can also upset this ecosystem. In the last century, as we humans have settled on the land, built homes and other permanent structures, and gotten attached to the look of certain places provided by the plants that grow there, we've done everything we can to suppress fires. But fires are a naturally occurring part of nature. Grasslands tolerate fire well—the foliage may go, but the roots survive and the plants fully recover within three years. Without periodic fire, trees and shrubs

MEALS FOR THE ROAD

BEFORE THE RAILROAD came to Southeastern Arizona, travelers considered themselves lucky if the stagecoach stops could offer beans and clean water. Beef and biscuits were a luxury.

The dining options in Southeastern Arizona have improved, but they're not as abundant as in more thickly settled areas. If you're heading off for a day of exploration, plan ahead and consider when you're likely to get hungry and where you'll eat. Some of the most beautiful scenery is an hour or more away from any restaurant.

If you're planning to go hiking or visit a park or nature preserve, taking a picnic is the best idea. You'll find sandwich shops in most small towns as well as the familiar fast food outlets in Sierra Vista and at the junction of Interstate 10 and AZ Hwy. 90. You'll want to stock up here for Kartchner Caverns.

During Tombstone's boom years in the 1880s, newspapers reported that the town had the best restaurants between St. Louis and San Francisco. They served fresh oysters, lobster, and prime rib—an entire meal for about 25 cents. Such elegant dining is scarce in the area today, but many family-friendly spots serve up tasty portions of steaks, hamburgers, and Mexican food.

If you're from out of the region, don't worry that all Mexican food is full of chiles that will burn your mouth. You can get it that way if you want, but you'll find many menu items that are both authentic and mild.

Vegetarians or travelers looking for fine dining will have the best luck in Sonoita and Bisbee, where artsy and well-heeled local residents support restaurants with eclectic menus. In Bisbee, the tables on the front porch of the Copper Queen Hotel are considered a prime people-watching perch. In Sonoita, you can accompany your meal with a wine from a local vineyard.

Other towns where you'll find restaurants are Benson, Tubac, and Douglas (the coffee shop in the Gadsden Hotel is a back-in-time experience). In Willcox, serious coffee drinkers can find an espresso fix in a small antique store across from City Hall. Willcox, with its abundance of fresh fruit, is a mecca for pie lovers.

When in doubt about where to stop for a bite, follow the Pickup Rule: If there are lots of pickup trucks parked outside, the food is probably pretty good. You'll find that the person who brings your food will be called a waitress, not a server, and there's a good chance she'll address you as "Hon."

And for dress? Shirts and shoes are required just about everywhere. Beyond that, pressed jeans and a clean shirt are considered dress-up wear.

Left Back, oil painting by Alysa Bennett of the 99 Bar Ranch, Douglas.

"The Island" picnic area of Roper Lake State Park near Safford. BERNADETTE HEATH

WHETHER YOU'RE CONSIDERING a short getaway or a week-long vacation, Southeastern Arizona has all the elements for a rewarding family experience. Here are some of the attractions where you can take your children or grandchildren and be sure they'll have a great time. In addition to the activities listed here, don't forget camping in the forest or fishing at any of the lakes, such as Patagonia Lake, where an 11-year-old boy still holds the world record for the largest green sunfish hybrid ever caught. (For more information, see page 26.)

Tombstone What child could resist a ride in a real stagecoach or wagon through the streets where Wyatt Earp and his brothers had their famous shoot-out? During Tombstone's frequent special events, kids can mingle with lawmen and outlaws in Old West dress. (For more about Tombstone, see page 37.)

Kartchner Caverns Youngsters will marvel at the colorful underground rooms and spooky black tunnels that lead to the unexplored regions. The museum has well-designed exhibits that make learning fun. Children must be able to walk, as no strollers are allowed underground. (For more about Kartchner Caverns, see page 42.)

Bisbee On the Queen Mine Tour, you'll don slickers, hard hats, and battery-pack headlamps for a trip in converted ore carts deep into the dark tunnels where miners once labored to extract copper. Retired miners give tours and explain how they worked. Winter and summer, it's just 47° 1,800 feet underground. Dress warmly. (For more about Bisbee, see page 40.)

Tubac Presidio State Historic Park Even in territorial times children needed an education, and the museum includes a replica of an early schoolhouse. On weekends from October through March, volunteers dress in period costume for a living history exhibit, giving a glimpse of how the settlers in Tubac raised and cooked their food and fashioned a life in the Old West. (For more about Tubac Presidio State Historic Park, see page 18.)

Tumacácori National Historic Park A Junior Ranger program and treasure hunt help youngsters explore the park. Ask about both at the front desk. Be sure to watch the video, which gives a look at what life was like for Indian children at the mission. During the December fiesta, many activities are geared specifically to children. (For more about Tumacácori, see page 17.)

Discovery Park in Safford In addition to looking at the night sky through a large telescope, children will enjoy a *Star Trek*-like journey in Discovery Park's state-of-the-art space simulator named Shuttlecraft Polaris. A narrow-gauge railway encircles the park. (For more about Discovery Park, see page 68.)

The Slaughter Ranch John Slaughter was a famous sheriff of Cochise County, and his ranch, outside Douglas, was almost a town in itself. An ice house shows how the Slaughters kept things cold before refrigeration, and a Model-T Ford is parked in a garage. If youngsters get restless while the grownups are looking at the photo displays, there's plenty of room to run around, or they can watch videos of movies in which Sheriff Slaughter appears as a character. (For more about Slaughter Ranch, see page 61.)

Chiricahua National Monument The towering cliffs and hoodoos in Chiricahua National Monument should bring an awed "Cool!" even from children otherwise blasé regarding the beauty of this extraordinary landscape. Well-marked trails lead you into the heart of the totem-like spires. A stop at Faraway Ranch, an early guest ranch, will interest older children. (For more about Chiricahua National Monument, see page 64.)

Amerind Foundation Museum Native Americans inhabited Southeastern Arizona for thousands of years before white settlers arrived. Older youngsters will enjoy the exhibits. School tours are popular and must be scheduled in advance. (For more about the Amerind Foundation, see page 66.)

Gammons Gulch It's not a real Old West town, but the Gammons Gulch movie set, just north of Benson, has all the elements of a late-1880s ghost town. Visitors can explore the buildings, which include a blacksmith shop and saloon. (For more about Gammons Gulch, see page 50.)

take over grasslands, and that is exactly what has happened in much of what had been vast sweeps of range grasses in Southeastern Arizona.

We see the effects of fire suppression also in the forests—formerly they were much more open, with bigger trees and grass between them. When fire raged through, it killed the small seedlings and rejuvenated the grass while the older trees had bark thick enough to protect them. These days the upper-elevation forests are thick with smaller trees. During a big fire—one that gets away from the firefighters and cannot be stopped—the smaller trees provide fuel that makes a much hotter fire that kills the older trees.

Sky Islands

Sky islands are forest-studded mountain ranges that are isolated from each other by surrounding valleys of grasslands or desert scrub. In Southeastern Arizona, we find these high-elevation atolls in the Santa Rita, Galiuro, Huachuca, and Chiricahua mountain ranges. Mount Graham in the Pinaleños is one of the best-known sky islands.

As you climb these mountains of Southeastern Arizona, you pass through a succession of plant communities. Every thousand feet in elevation you climb is the equivalent of moving 300 miles north. Between 6,000 and 7,000 feet, you enter ponderosa pine forest. Around 7,500 feet, firs become the predominant trees, and above 9,000 feet you'll begin to see subalpine forests of Englemann spruce and fir trees. Even in dry years, these lofty mountains usually receive some snowfall, and the runoff from spring snowmelt and summer rains water lush vegetation in the canyons.

Because they include so many different ecological zones, the sky islands support a broad range of species of plants, animals, and insects. However, these "islands" are often too small to permit the ecological processes that would take place in larger areas and too isolated for the natural migration of animals and plants among the islands. Living things adapted to the cooler and wetter conditions of the mountains cannot survive while traversing drier areas. Fences, roads, and housing developments make passage even more difficult.

Isolated sky islands are particularly difficult for large mammals such as bears and wolves that need to range widely to breed.

Everything in an ecosystem is connected. The numbers of songbirds, for example, have declined since we've gotten rid of large carnivores such as wolves and cougars. The carnivores used to eat the raccoons, foxes, skunks, and opossums that are now heavily dining on songbird eggs.

Natural Beauty at Risk

Interest in conservation in Southeastern Arizona goes back decades, but it has become more intense lately. The natural beauty of the region, its open space, and all its plants and animals could be easily lost to us and to future generations by overdevelopment. Right after the beginning

A bigtooth maple tree in the South Fork of Cave Creek, Chiricahua Wilderness, once part of the hunting grounds of the Chiricahua Apache.
LARRY ULRICH

of the 20th century, most of Southeastern Arizona's mountain ranges became national forests. In 1917 they were consolidated into the Coronado National Forest.

These areas are still protected, but open range that once stretched for miles—with nothing but cactus, cows, and the occasional stock tank—now sprouts homes. The water table is being drawn down for dishwashers, swimming pools, and golf courses, threatening the natural waterways on which the plants and animals depend.

There is greater public awareness today that, without planning, the region's natural resources could be overused and degraded beyond recovery. In response to this wake-up call, ecologically minded citizens, including ranchers and outdoor enthusiasts, have joined with business leaders and government agents to preserve all that makes Southeastern Arizona such a wonderful place to live and to visit.

Different factions come to the table with long-standing mistrust. Many ecologists view cattle as nothing but an invading, non-native species responsible for a long list of depredations on the land. Some ranchers fume that the scientists and save-the-land types are nosy, do-gooding latecomers and have no business sticking their noses into the ranchers' traditional way of life. But over years of talks and compromise, the different groups are helping to forge a consensus on the best approach to preservation. Among the results is the establishment of the 42,000-acre Las Cienegas National Conservation Area, which protects the area around the historic Empire Ranch and Cienega Creek and much of the high desert grasslands of the Sonoita Valley.

One way that land can be preserved from development and sprawl is through conservation easements, which ranchers and other people who own large pieces of property may opt to convey. This is how an easement works: Every piece of property includes a group of rights—mineral, water, hunting, grazing, and development. A conservation easement is a legal agreement that permanently transfers one or more of these rights to a qualified party—such as The Nature Conservancy—while the property owners retain the right to live on the land and use it more or less as they did before, and to sell the land with the rights they have retained. Ranchers receive some tax benefits and the satisfaction of helping to preserve a way of life to which most are deeply committed.

THE
SOUNDTRACK
FOR YOUR TRIP

IN SOUTHEASTERN ARIZONA the radio stations reflect the culture of the region, particularly its taste for Country Western music. On local stations, you'll hear a lot of George Strait, Martina McBride, and Waylon Jennings, often singing ballads or other songs that deal with patriotism, childhood memories, sweethearts won and lost, and the general pain of life. Listening to these songs as you drive through the region will give you an appropriate soundtrack for your experience.

Close to the international border, your car radio will also pull in a number of Mexican stations. Along with the pop songs of the moment, you'll hear what's called *Norteño* music. This is the traditional sound of the area and an integral part of the lives of the rural people of northern Mexico. It includes a button accordion, a *bajo*

Apache Pass Road, leading from Chiricahua National Monument to Fort Bowie. LARRY LINDAHL

sexto or 12-string guitar, and usually an electric bass and drums. More than a century ago, Germans who came to work in the Mexican breweries brought the

Oak trees, San Rafael Valley. J. KEITH SCHREIBER

Down by Douglas, forward-looking ranchers have formed their own conservation association, the Malpai Borderlands Group. They hold conservation easements given by ranchers in return for the privilege of using other rangelands when they need to move their cattle off their own land temporarily.

accordion to the area, and *Norteño* songs often have a polka beat and the brassy sound of an oompah band.

Norteño music may have an imported rhythm, but the lyrics are lively, passionate, and all Mexican. Many of the songs are ballads called *corridos* and tell of historic events, bandits, horses, shoot-outs, drug trafficking and, of course, love gone right and wrong. Some historians believe *corridos* are descended from pre-Hispanic epic poetry.

You can hear Country Western and *Norteño* music live in bars or at fairs and festivals in the region, usually on weekends. Dolan Ellis, Arizona's official balladeer for more than 30 years, performs original music every Saturday and Sunday afternoon at the Arizona Folklore Preserve, 44 Ramsey Canyon Rd. (six miles south of Sierra Vista on AZ Hwy. 92, then 3½ miles up Ramsey Canyon Rd.). You must make reservations for the shows at 520-378-6165.

Wave When You Pass

Today Southeastern Arizona is home to a mix of artists, military personnel, business people, ranchers, and retirees. As you drive the highways away from the towns, there are few houses in view. But look where the dirt roads go off into the distance, and you'll see rows of mailboxes. People move out here to have space and don't care if they have to drive five miles to get their mail or 50 miles to a decent grocery store. Most folks are very friendly—they stop for you if you have car trouble, look for you all night if you get hurt or lost while hiking, and wave at you when you pass on a dirt road. It is considered good manners to wave back. Those individualists who chose to live in Southeastern Arizona like their neighbors—they just don't want them too close.

Out here, people work hard, but nobody is getting rich. That's not to say that there aren't plenty of well-off people, but practically all of them made their money elsewhere. To the casual observer, it's hard to tell the rich from those who are barely scraping by. Drop in at the nearest bar or coffee shop, and you'll see pretty much everybody wearing a Western hat with a

LIGHTS! CAMERA! ACTION!

SOME FIRST-TIME VISITORS to Southeastern Arizona find that the area looks remarkably familiar. Those mountains, the grasslands, the yuccas—where have you seen them before? In the movies, of course.

The state of Oklahoma may be a very beautiful place—but if you've seen the sweep of that vast land only in the Gordon McRae and Shirley Jones movie named after the state, you haven't seen Oklahoma, you've seen the San Rafael Valley. That's where the musical was filmed in 1955.

Here are some of the other movies made in Southeastern Arizona. Several episodes of the television shows *Bonanza*, *The Young Riders*, *Gunsmoke*, and *The Young Pioneers* were also filmed in the area, as were many commercials.

John Wayne and Montgomery Clift in the movie *Red River*.

MOVIE	ACTORS	YEAR	LOCATION
Red River	John Wayne, Montgomery Clift	1948	Elgin
Duel in the Sun	Gregory Peck, Joseph Cotton	1948	Sonoita
Oklahoma!	Gordon MacRae, Shirley Jones	1955	San Rafael Valley
3:10 to Yuma	Glenn Ford, Van Heflin	1957	Elgin
The Big Country	Gregory Peck, Charlton Heston	1958	San Rafael Valley
Hombre	Paul Newman	1958	Greaterville
Last Train from Gun Hill	Kirk Douglas	1958	Elgin/Patagonia
Hour of the Gun	James Garner	1959	Sonoita/Elgin
The Wild Rovers	William Holden	1960	San Rafael Valley
Cimarron	Glenn Ford, Anne Baxter	1960	Mescal, Benson
McLintock	John Wayne, Maureen O'Hara	1963	San Rafael Valley
Monte Walsh	Lee Marvin	1970	Sonoita/Elgin
The Cowboys	John Wayne	1970	Sonoita/Elgin
Tom Horn	Steve McQueen	1982	San Rafael Valley
Cold Feet	Keith Carradine	1989	Naco/Bisbee
Young Guns II	Kiefer Sutherland, Christian Slater	1990	Tumacácori/Willcox Playa
Red Rock West	Nicolas Cage	1992	Willcox
Pontiac Moon	Ted Danson	1994	Douglas/Benson/Sonoita
Wyatt Earp: Return to Tombstone	Hugh O'Brien	1994	Tombstone
Tin Cup	Kevin Costner	1996	Tubac Golf Resort
Traffic	Benicio Del Toro, Michael Douglas	2000	Nogales
Groom Lake	William Shatner, Dan Gauthier	2001	Douglas, Bisbee

sweat-stained hatband and complaining about trouble with a well, a cat that got snatched by a coyote, or the need to take the pickup in for a brake job.

Waves of cultures have flourished in Southeastern Arizona for thousands of years, and then vanished to be replaced by yet other people with other customs. The influences of Western European civilization have been shaping the area for not quite 500 years. This latest culture, which has occupied the region for the shortest time, has affected the land the most profoundly. Unwilling to share their tasty beef with natural predators, early ranchers killed off most of the mountain lions and wolves. Now, when bears roam out of their allotted space in the deep forest, people kill them, too. During cycles when the streams dry up, we humans don't migrate; we dig wells, and then we dig them deeper. Pumping the wells lowers the water table, and streams become dry beds of sand.

Five hundred years is but a blip on Southeastern Arizona's evolutionary scale, and it may well be hubris to think that our culture will be the last to inhabit this land.

Rich in Potential Discoveries

Whether your passion is Old West history or enjoying unspoiled nature through hiking, stargazing, or bird-watching, you can find plenty of fascinating places to explore in Southeastern Arizona.

The following chapters are organized around the major valleys and their watersheds and mountain ranges: the missions and grasslands of the Santa Cruz and San Rafael Valleys, the mining towns and rich natural diversity of the San Pedro Valley, and the Apache homelands in the Sulphur Springs Valley and the Pinaleño and Chiricahua Mountains.

Discoveries await you—a breathtaking view of golden granite spires as your car tops a hill; a perfect streamside picnic site in a deep, shady canyon; and the glimpse of a violet-crowned hummingbird flitting among the mesquites along the San Pedro River. There is enough here to keep you busy for a month or a lifetime.

A winter storm over the Santa Rita Mountains and the mesquite-covered grasslands of Madera Canyon.
RANDY PRENTICE

PRESERVING YOUR TRIP
WITH PHOTOS

SOUTHEASTERN ARIZONA abounds in photogenic spots. Whether you're a serious hobbyist or a point-and-shooter, you'll be tempted to whip out your camera at every stop. But here's the deal about Arizona's clear, bright sun and deep blue sky — it's not so good for photography. If you take a picture of that scene that looks so wonderful to your eye when you stop for lunch at noon, you'll find that the shadows are black and the colors are washed out. Wait until late afternoon when the light is less harsh, or get out shortly after sunrise.

Don't take all wide-angle shots. Look for telling details: a steep staircase in Bisbee, a broken wagon wheel on the outskirts of Tombstone, the corner of a crumbling building in a ghost town.

As for those marvelous pictures of sunsets you see on postcards and in magazines, professional photographers will tell you getting the perfect shot is part skill and part luck. Colorful sunsets appear only on days when there are clouds, haze, or dust in the atmosphere. When you do get an evening sky splashed with orange, pink, and magenta, be prepared to take lots of shots as the colors will change quickly — there's no way to tell if in the next moment they'll be brighter or begin to fade.

Missions & Grasslands

Evening falls on agaves, grasslands, and the
Mustang Mountains, near Elgin. RANDY PRENTICE

2. ON A GOOD YEAR, a year when just the right amount of rain falls, the Santa Cruz River flows quietly north until it goes underground above Tubac. The river begins in the springs and marshes in the San Rafael Valley, flows south into Mexico, and then makes a sharp turn to the north. After a few miles, it is joined by Sonoita Creek and later by Madera Creek. The Santa Cruz waters the grass along its banks and the cottonwoods that provide shade and define the valley from miles away. From its upper reaches and all along its path, it supports large mammals such as bears, deer, and mountain lions along with rare frogs and salamanders and three native species of fish.

In dry years, the flow of the Santa Cruz might be reduced to only a trickle. But when heavy storms send torrents tumbling off the nearby Santa Rita Mountains, the river can rage outside its banks with strength sufficient to uproot even mature cottonwoods and hurl them as far as the desert north of Tucson, where the river spreads over the land and once again seeps beneath the ground.

Santa Cruz Valley

For centuries, ancestors of the modern Tohono O'odham Indians have lived near the Santa Cruz River. Jesuit missionary Eusebio Francisco Kino first visited these peaceful Piman farmers in 1691 and

later established missions at Guevavi, Calabasas, and Tumacácori. Father Kino also brought Old World crops and livestock. The introduction of winter wheat particularly won the Indians' gratitude as previously they had raised only corn, beans, and squash, which needed the warmth of summer to grow. Wheat could grow during the winter with its mild days but chilly and sometimes freezing nights.

It took decades for the missions to receive a resident priest, but, except for sporadic Apache raids, life proceeded more or less peacefully until 1751, when a brief Pima uprising led to the deaths of two priests and about 100 Spanish settlers, and wiped out Tubac, a small ranch about five miles north of Tumacácori. The next year, Spain established El Presidio de Tubac to protect the colonists and missionaries. It became Arizona's first European settlement.

Thinking that the presidio might offer some defense, and attracted by the rich grasslands southeast of Tubac, a few Spanish ranchers began running cattle in an area they called Pimería Alta—an area encompassing present-day Southern Arizona and northern Sonora, Mexico. But the Apaches were becoming much stronger and fiercer. They relentlessly attacked and raided anything and anybody in what they considered their area. By 1762 the ranchers had given up and left. Even the other Indians in the valley had had enough of the constant depredations and moved to the west.

The residents of Tubac and Tumacácori saw a great flurry of activity in October 1775. Juan Bautista de Anza II, commander of the presidio, arrived with 177 people, 1,000 head of cattle, horses, and mules, and more than eight tons of food and equipment, all heading to California. Sixty-three people from Tubac elected to join the expedition that culminated in the founding of San Francisco. The next year, Spain decided to move the presidio from Tubac to Tucson, leaving the priests at Tumacácori to cope with hostile Indians alone until the presidio was reactivated 11 years later.

We read that in 1800 the Franciscans of the Mission of San José de Tumacácori began building the church we see today. In fact, while the priests may have planned and directed the construction,

the Indians did the labor over the 22 years it took to complete the building and paint it brilliantly in bold red, blue, green, and yellow. It functioned for only 18 years. In 1840, demoralized by constant Apache attacks on the residents and the livestock, the priests abandoned Tumacácori. In 1844, the mission and surrounding property were auctioned to someone who started a woolen factory, using the land to graze 10,000 sheep and 600 goats before abandoning the site in 1855.

For more than half a century, the church stood alone with only the sounds of nature replacing the former hubbub of the mission community. And yet, when the building became a national monument in 1908, frescoes in the front of the church were still visible. Today three conservators from Mexico City keep them fresh. Whenever flakes fall from the frescoes, they are carefully saved and glued back with a substance made from the prickly pear cactus, which helps in the preservation.

La Fiesta de Tumacácori is held the first weekend in December. Although the church has been deconsecrated, two high masses are held there each year, usually in April and October. Only a hundred people are allowed into the church at a time, and all those who attend are asked to dress in period costume. On Christmas Eve, the church and the paths are lit with 2,000 softly glowing *luminarias*.

While the mission property was undergoing ownership changes, Tubac was also abandoned and resettled several times. After Tubac became American territory, it was occupied by the developers of the Sonora Exploring and Mining Company, headed by Charles D. Poston. In 1859 Poston established Arizona's first newspaper there.

The artist colony of Tubac also offers a bounty of goods from Mexico for shoppers.
CAROLYN NEITHAMMER

The old Tubac Schoolhouse is now part of Tubac Presidio State Historic Park. RANDY PRENTICE

Reliable water, tall cottonwoods, mountain views, and abundant sunshine and economic opportunity attracted inhabitants, and by 1860 the tiny adobe village by the river had grown into the largest town in Arizona. Poston called it a community "in a perfect state of nature," and he frequently relaxed in shady pools in the Santa Cruz River as he read his newspaper. However, the company failed to make money, the Civil War drained the area of protection from the Apaches, and the population declined.

For the last half century, Tubac has increasingly attracted artists and craftspeople and is today a thriving art colony with galleries and shops. You can learn more about the long and colorful past of the village in the museum at Tubac Presidio State Historic Park.

If you have time, plan to hike along the 4½-mile stretch of the Juan Bautista de Anza National Historic Trail that runs between Tubac and Tumacácori. The trail crosses the river several times, so plan to get your feet wet. Educational ramadas explain the cultural and ecological history. Birders should find plenty to interest them; a study in 2000, for example, found many breeding pairs of the endangered yellow-billed cuckoos in the cottonwoods and willows along this section of the trail. Another five-mile section of the trail starts just north of Rio Rico Drive (Interstate 19 exit 17), where it intersects with the Santa Cruz River. The two sections of the shady trail will eventually be linked. Long-range plans call for the trail to continue all the way from Nogales, Arizona, to San Francisco, tracing more or less the path De Anza and his party followed in 1775-76.

Tumacácori National Historic Park Open daily 8 a.m.-5 p.m., except Thanksgiving and Christmas. Rangers periodically lead tours to the Calabasas and Guevavi mission ruins. Admission: adults $2, families $4. To reach Tumacácori Mission from Tucson, drive south on I-19 about 40 miles, take exit 29, and drive south to 1891 E. Frontage Road. For further information, call 520-398-2341 or visit www.nps.gov/tuma.

Tubac Presidio State Historic Park Open daily 8 a.m.-5 p.m., except Christmas. Every Sunday afternoon, Oct.-Mar., Los Tubaqueños volunteer living history program reenacts life in the Spanish Colonial era. Admission: adults $2, children 7-13 $1, children 6 and under free. From Tucson, drive south on I-19 about 35 miles to exit 34, then drive south about one mile. For further information, call 520-398-2252 or visit www.pr.state.az.us/parkhtml/tubac.html. The web address for the Tubac Chamber of Commerce is www.tubacaz.com.

Nogales

Toward the southern edge of the Santa Cruz Valley and straddling the international border are the sister towns of Nogales, Arizona, and Nogales, Sonora. The communities were founded in 1880 when two merchants pitched tents on either side of the border in an area named for the grove of walnut trees (*nogales*) that grew in a wet area nearby. For many years border crossings were very casual, and one story tells of an early saloon that had one door opening to the United States and another to Mexico. Today the Arizona community remains a small town with a population of less than 30,000, while the Mexican Nogales has grown to 300,000.

You can learn about the history of *Ambos Nogales* (both Nogaleses) in three museums in Nogales, Arizona. The Pimería Alta Historical Society, in the former city hall and fire station, has displays as well as a research library with historic photographs and documents. The Santa Cruz Cowbelles Western Heritage Center and the Arizona Rangers Museum, both small, are in the 1904 county court house, a national landmark. At the historical society or the

Afternoon light falls on rolling hills around the two border towns of Nogales, Arizona, and Nogales, Sonora. RANDY PRENTICE

A deserted Santa Cruz County road below the San Cayetano Mountains. RANDY PRENTICE

visitor kiosk on the border, pick up a map for self-guided tours (two walking and one driving) that will take you past some of Nogales' elegant homes and interesting commercial buildings.

Should you get the urge to blend in with Southeastern Arizona locals—at least as far as footwear is concerned—a Nogales, Arizona, business worth a visit is the Paul Bond Boot Company, headed by its namesake, who has been crafting boots since 1929.

Paul Bond boots are worn by both working cowboys—who tend to buy the basic $450 calfskin style—and such Western celebrities as Johnny Cash, Barbara Mandrell, Randy Travis, and Dwight Yoakam—who prefer the more elaborate versions. These are made of exotic leathers such as kangaroo and ostrich, with fanciful designs on the shaft, at prices upwards of $2,000. Visitors are welcome to visit the factory at 915 W. Paul Bond Dr. off West Mariposa Drive, whether to buy, to wish, or just be amazed at the display of "boot art."

A Nogales enterprise most North Americans have benefited from without knowing it is the transport of fresh produce. More than a third of the winter fruits and vegetables consumed in the U.S. pass through Nogales from the Mexican fields where they are grown to northern dinner tables. From the highway you can see large warehouses and refrigerated trucks getting ready to head out with lettuce and melons

that will soon be displayed in neighborhood grocery stores from Ohio to Seattle.

Thousands of people every day walk across the border to shop in Nogales, Sonora, for good buys on brightly colored pottery, leather goods, jewelry, and crafts from other Mexican states. The busy marketplace makes for great entertainment even if you do nothing but window shop. Only a few years ago, it seemed as though every fourth store sold liquor, but many of them have been converted to pharmacies where Arizonans flock to get prescription drugs at discounted rates. If you are a U.S. citizen, you should have a passport or voter registration card and photo identification; nationals of other countries should take their passports and double-check with customs officials before crossing.

If you find yourself in Mexico at mealtime, stop for lunch or dinner at one of the many excellent restaurants. Two favorites are Elvira's at the corner of Obregón and Internacional, where each customer is served a complimentary shot of tequila with fresh lime, or the elegant La Roca, to the east of the rail line and main highway on Calle Elías.

Pimería Alta Historical Society 136 N. Grand Ave., Nogales, AZ. Open Friday 10 a.m.–5 p.m., Saturday 10 a.m–4 p.m., and Sunday 1–4 p.m. The research library is open daily. Admission is free. Call 520-287-4621.

Santa Cruz Cowbelles Western Heritage Center and Arizona Rangers Museum Old Court House, 405 N. Morley Ave., Nogales, AZ. Open the first Saturday of the month. Visit www.azrangers.org/museum.htm.

Paul Bond Boot Company 915 W. Paul Bond Dr., off West Mariposa Drive, Nogales, AZ. Open Monday through Saturday, 8 a.m.–5 p.m. Call 520-281-0512 or visit www.paulbondboots.net.

WINE COUNTRY

THE TINY SETTLEMENT OF ELGIN lies at the northern edge of the San Rafael Valley—a land of cattle raising and beer drinking, at least until the late 1970s.

Gordon Dutt, then a soil specialist and professor at the University of Arizona, was working on a grant to find new agricultural lands and products that would grow in Arizona's climate and not use too much water.

In an area near Elgin in the Sonoita Valley, Dutt and his colleagues found a spot oddly perfect for growing wine grapes. The 5,000-foot elevation helps to create the warm days and cool nights needed to grow fruit with the ideal sugar-to-acid ratio for premium wines. The soil, surprisingly similar to that of the best wine-growing regions of Burgundy in France, is called *terra rossa*—"red earth." It is loamy and acidic on the surface, with red clay beneath that and soil rich in lime on the bottom.

Sonoita Vineyards grape harvest, Elgin. GILL C. KENNY

Merlot handmade from grapes grown by winemaker Leo Cox. And farther to the east, Dos Cabezas Wineworks in Kansas Settlement, just south of Willcox, produces award-winning Petite Sirahs and Chardonnays and what some call the best Sangiovese made in America. Colibri Vineyards, the latest addition to the field, is located on a former orchard near Portal in the Chiricahua Mountains. Colibri had its first harvest in 2002.

You'll find some products from these wineries termed Appellation Sonoita, which means that 100% of the grapes used were grown in the Sonoita Valley. Others will be Appellation Cochise, indicating that the grapes came from Cochise County, a wider area that includes vineyards in Bowie, Kansas Settlement, and Portal.

Dutt made wine from the first grapes he grew there. Despite his inexperience as a winemaker, some of his early efforts were pretty good. He then started Sonoita Vineyards, where he could grow enough grapes for a small commercial operation, planting his vines widely spaced on a terraced hillside to take advantage of every drop of rain. Supplemental water is provided by drip irrigation. Dutt also got some lessons in the fine points of the vintner's art, and by 1989 Sonoita Valley's Cabernet was among the American regional wines served at the senior George Bush's presidential inauguration. Today, Dutt's wines are consistent award-winners.

The Sonoita Vineyard has now been joined by several other wineries in the Elgin area. Callaghan Vineyards has 17 acres planted in about a dozen different varieties of grapes in its Buena Suerte Vineyard in Elgin and also uses grapes from a vineyard near Willcox. The Callaghan wines have won many awards and have been served at White House state dinners. The Village of Elgin Winery is located in a historic building in the center of the town. The grapes for Village of Elgin Wine Companies, crushed by the traditional foot-stomping method, have won numerous awards.

North of Elgin, off the Sonoita Highway, a smaller winery called Charron Vineyards specializes in White

Callaghan Vineyards on Elgin Road off AZ Hwy. 83, 336 Elgin Road, Elgin, AZ 85611, 520-455-5322 or www.callaghanvineyards.com. Tasting room open Fri.-Sun. 11 a.m.–3 p.m.

Charron Vineyards 18585 South Sonoita Highway, Vail, AZ 85641, 520-762-8585 or www.charronvineyards.com. Call or e-mail for hours and directions.

Colibri Vineyards at the end of White Tail Canyon, 2825 Hilltop Road, Portal, AZ 85632, 520-558-2401 or www.colibrivineyard.com. Call for an appointment.

Dos Cabezas Wineworks just south of Willcox, 19-B Wayward Winds Road, off Robbs Road, Kansas Settlement, AZ 85643, 520-455-5369. Call for hours and directions.

Sonoita Vineyards south of AZ Hwy. 82 on Elgin/Canelo Road, HC1, Box 33, Elgin, AZ 85611, 520-455-5893 or www.sonoitavineyards.com. Tasting room open daily 10 a.m.–4 p.m.

The Village of Elgin Winery in the heart of Elgin on AZ Hwy. 82, 471 Elgin Road, Elgin, AZ 85611, 520-455-9309 or www.earl-of-ellam.com (click "wine estates," then "Village of Elgin Winery"). Tasting room open daily 10 a.m.–5 p.m., except Christmas.

Madera Canyon

Hollywood's finest set designer could not have come up with a more stunning backdrop for the Santa Cruz Valley than the soaring Santa Rita Mountains. The best access to the Santa Ritas is through cool, shady Madera Canyon.

Madera Canyon is a mecca for bird-watchers, who come to observe the hundreds of species that visit the area, including an impressive selection of hummingbirds. More than 100 species of birds breed in this lush byway, including the elegant trogon, the painted red start, and elf and whiskered screech owls. The feeding station at the Santa Rita Lodge is open to the public, and the lodge conducts regular morning bird walks.

You will find an extensive series of hiking trails leading from the parking area where the road dead-ends. Many of the trails are short, while others are longer and involve considerable climbing. If you are fond of long-distance views, head up the five-mile trail to Josephine Saddle, or if you're a really hardy trekker, go all the way to the top of Mount Wrightson.

As you drive in, you may see signs for the Santa Rita Experimental Range. Founded in 1903, and operated by the Forest Service and the University of Arizona, this is the oldest research area of its kind. Scientists use the 53,000 acres of semiarid grasslands to conduct long-term studies on issues such as storm runoff, erosion, and changes in vegetation over time.

Madera Canyon Open daily. Entrance fee: $5/vehicle. Campsites: $10/night. No reservations. Bird walks at Santa Rita Lodge: $12/person. From Tucson, drive south on I-19 and take exit 63, Continental Road. Drive east, toward the Santa Rita Mountains, and follow White House Canyon Road to Madera Canyon Road. The distance from the freeway to the parking lot is about 15 miles. For further information, call 520-281-2296 or visit www.fs.fed.us/r3/coronado/nrd/madera/madera_canyon. For reservations at the Santa Rita Lodge, call 520-625-8746 or point your browser to www.santaritalodge.com.

Male broad-billed hummingbird.
TOM VEZO

Painted bunting.
TOM VEZO

Montezuma quail.
TOM VEZO

Female summer tanager.
TOM VEZO

Sam and Mac Donaldson of the Empire Ranch (second- and third-generation Arizona ranchers) at the first Sonoita Ranch Horse Competition.   W. ROSS HUMPHREYS

Empire Ranch

The fabled Empire Ranch made its owners rich from both ranching and mining. When many other ranchers in Southeastern Arizona were just barely hanging on to livelihoods from small herds of cattle, Walter L. Vail was a shrewd entrepreneur. In 1876, he and a partner bought 160 acres, a small adobe house and corral, and 612 head of cattle just north of today's Sonoita. After learning that they had silver on their property, they operated the Total Wreck mine on the northern part of the ranch between 1880 and 1885. By 1905, the Empire Ranch covered 1,000 square miles and supported vast herds of cattle and sheep.

After Vail sold the ranch in 1928, it passed through several owners. It was sold in 1960 for real-estate development and subsequently to a mining company for its water rights and mineral potential. Fortunately for the preservation of the landscape, a series of land exchanges brought the property into public ownership,

and the Bureau of Land Management now administers it as part of Las Cienegas National Conservation Area.

In many places, you'll notice the grasses growing as tall as your head, giving an idea of what this part of the country looked like in its pristine state. Ranchers who hold leases for cattle grazing are still working the land. They have won awards for their sensitive management, and the state of the range is testimony to their care for it. These healthy grasslands are home to abundant wildlife, including more than 170 species of deer, birds, and pronghorn antelope. The animals are supported by a riparian area formed by the year-round flow of Cienega Creek, which meanders shallowly for about 10 miles beginning about three miles east of the ranch house. "Cienega" is the Spanish word for marsh, and numerous wetlands lie along the creek.

On the way into the ranch, you'll pass the ranch house and outbuildings. Unoccupied since the 1970s,

GOLFING

SOUTHEASTERN ARIZONA IS GOLFER'S HEAVEN. You might not find as much grass as on courses in wetter areas, and in winter the grass might not be deep green, but the sky will be blue, the sun warm, and the surrounding view inspiring.

Male lazuli bunting.
TOM VEZO

Douglas Municipal Golf Course 22 Fairway Dr., Douglas, AZ 85607, 520-364-3722. 18 holes. Open to the public. Mature trees shade the front nine while the back is newer with desert mesquite trees that add challenge.

Kino Springs Golf Club 187 Kino Springs Dr., Nogales, AZ 85621, 800-732-5751. 18 holes. Some tee times open to the public. A forgiving course that lies along a riverbed outside Nogales.

Mountain View Golf Course Bldg. 15479, Ft. Huachuca, AZ 85670, 520-533-7088, 520-533-7092 for tee times. 18 holes. Also has a snack bar, driving range, and putting green.

Palo Duro Creek Golf Course 2690 N. Country Club Dr., Nogales, AZ 85621, 520-761-4394. 18 holes. Some tee times open to the public. Well-maintained grass fairways with the bonus of great views.

Pueblo del Sol Country Club 2770 S. Saint Andrews Dr., Sierra Vista, AZ 85650, 520-803-9913. 18 holes. Some tee times open to the public. Meticulously manicured greens and fairways make this a popular course.

Rio Rico Resort & Country Club 1069 Camino Caralampi, Rio Rico, AZ 85648, 800-288-4746, 520-281-1901. 18 holes. Some tee times open to the public. Picturesque fairways are lined with mesquite, cottonwood, pine, and willow trees.

Shadow Mountain Country Club 1105 Irene St., Pearce, AZ 85625 , 520-826-3412. 18 holes. Open to the public.

Tubac Golf Resort 1 Otero Road, Tubac, AZ 85646, 520-398-2211. 18 holes. Priority to members and guests. Mature cottonwood trees grow along the Santa Cruz River, making the area bordering the course appear particularly lush. This is the former site of the Otero cattle ranch.

Turquoise Hills Family Golf Center 800 E. Country Club Rd., Benson, AZ 85602, 520-586-2585. 18 holes. Open to the public. Also has a barbecue area and RV spaces.

Turquoise Valley Golf Course 1791 W. Newell St., Naco, AZ 85620, 520-432-3091. 18 holes. Open to the public. Right on the Mexican border, the course features wide fairways and tall trees on the first nine holes, dating from the 1930s. The back nine offer a more deserty contrast.

Twin Lakes Municipal Golf Course 1000 S. Rex Allen Jr. Dr., Willcox, Arizona 85643, 520-384-2720. 9 holes. Open to the public. You can combine golf with bird-watching as the surrounding area supports diverse wildlife.

Tubac Golf Resort.

the house is in poor condition and is being stabilized. When Vail bought the ranch, there were just three small adobe rooms, and you'll see those in a line to the north. The more recent additions include a half-hexagon bay window Vail ordered for his wife as a wedding present when he brought her to the ranch from New Jersey. She must have liked it there, because they stayed and reared seven children.

The ranch is open to all who want to experience its pristine natural setting by bird-watching, camping, hiking, horseback riding, bicycling, or picnicking. The roads are unpaved, and there are no developed facilities of any kind. You are free to look around the exterior of the ranch house and explore the tack room and adobe barn. The nonprofit Empire Ranch Foundation is raising money to restore the ranch house and to help with the historic interpretation of the Empire Ranch and rural life in Southeastern Arizona.

Violet-crowned hummingbird.
TOM VEZO

Las Cienegas National Conservation Area/Empire Ranch Open year-round. Free admission. Campers may stay 14 days within a six-month period. From Tucson, drive east on I-10 to AZ Hwy. 83 south. The sign that marks the turnoff to the Empire Cienega Resource Area is located about 25 miles south of I-10 and seven miles north of Sonoita on AZ Hwy. 83. From the turnoff, drive east about three miles to the ranch house. For further information, call 520-258-7200 or visit www.az.blm.gov/tfo/index.htm. The web address for the resource friends group is www.empireranchfoundation.org.

Sonoita Valley

During the years that Spain and Mexico ruled the area they called Pimería Alta, they dispensed enormous land grants of somewhat indeterminate boundaries. As part of the Gadsden Purchase in

1854, the Americans agreed to honor the grants, leaving the property in the hands of the families who had been there for years. Some of the ranches near Patagonia and Sonoita still carry the names of these original land grants.

When the United States took over the Sonoita Valley, the Apaches were still a threat, so the Army established Fort Buchanan and Fort Crittenden between 1857 and 1861 to help protect the settlers. Both forts were abandoned at the start of the Civil War and more than a million dollars' worth of military property was destroyed so that it could not be used by Confederate troops.

More people came to the area when word spread that the oak-dotted hills were extremely rich in minerals— silver, gold, lead, and copper. Legends tell of fortunes of pure silver taken from mines in the area during the time of the early Spanish missionaries. Whether this is true or not, we do know that in the 1800s mines such as Greaterville, Salero, Mowry, Harshaw, Washington Camp, and Duquesne produced enough to be economically successful. Extracting the ore was not without danger to the miners, however, despite the soldiers at the nearby forts. Two early American miners, John Wrightson and Gilbert Hopkins, worked the Salero Mine in the upper Santa Cruz valley. They did not live to enjoy their riches, however; Apaches killed both in 1860. They are remembered today in the names of two of the highest peaks in the Santa Ritas, Mount Wrightson and Mount Hopkins.

Sonoita & Patagonia

With the land delivering bountiful minerals and fat cattle, the miners and ranchers needed a way to move their products. The village of Sonoita sprang up when the Benson-to-Nogales Railway was put through in 1882. At first the railroad brought in cattle. Later, ranchers shipped as many as 3,000 head a day to East Coast markets.

Sonoita remains a major ranching center. Pickup trucks far outnumber passenger cars, and the rodeo grounds occupy the largest chunk of real estate in the center of town. Over the last few decades, however, non-ranchers have moved into the area to enjoy the pleasant climate and clean air. A small business community with first-rate restaurants has grown up at the crossroads of AZ Hwys. 82 and 83.

About 16 years after Sonoita was founded, Patagonia was established 12 miles to the west, straddling the railroad track. Ranchers and miners came to town to ship their cattle and ore, and Patagonia grew quickly with hotels and bars and even an opera house. As the mines closed down and the cattle business declined, many people left. But others moved in, attracted by the tranquil community atmosphere.

After the rails were torn up in 1962, the railway station became the Patagonia town hall, and the property around it shades a three-block-long park where the Fall Festival is held every October. Volunteers maintain a small section of the park as a garden that attracts more than 90 species of butterflies.

Male yellow-headed blackbirds resting among reeds.
TOM VEZO

Pick up a butterfly list from the nearby Kazzam Nature Center, and maybe you'll be lucky enough to see a black swallowtail, a western pygmy blue, or a silver-spotted skipper alighting for a nectar lunch.

Eden in the Desert

Sonoita Creek flows just north of the town and forms the main attraction for the Patagonia-Sonoita Creek Preserve, run by The Nature Conservancy. Trails wind through the shady 750-acre preserve, one of the richest of the few remaining streamside habitats in Southeastern Arizona. Gray hawks nest in the 100-foot tall Fremont cottonwoods that have stood guard over this creek for 130 years and are the oldest trees of their kind anywhere. Arizona black walnuts and Goodding willows also grow by the creek. The Nature Conservancy is working to restore native vegetation and is carefully monitoring ecological changes in this precious resource.

The preserve attracts about 30,000 visitors every year, and practically all of them arrive with binoculars. Serious birders come to spot such unusual species as the thick-billed kingbird, the violet-crowned hummingbird, or the rose-throated becard. This desert Eden is also home to mountain lions, bobcats, white-tailed deer, javelinas, coatimundis, coyotes, desert tortoises, and assorted snakes, toads, frogs, and fish.

If, after a visit to the preserve, you haven't seen quite enough birds, you can stop at Wallace and Marion Paton's place about halfway back to town. The Patons welcome more than 2,000 visitors a year who want to see the magnificent array of hummingbirds that visit their feeders and nectar gardens.

A few miles to the west, the Sonoita Creek has been dammed to form Patagonia Lake. The two-mile-long lake is stocked regularly with fish, and there's a marina with boats to rent, a beach for swimming, and camping spots that fill up by Friday

White-tailed deer buck, Mount Graham. WALT ANDERSON

night on summer weekends. It's not unusual to see a great blue heron wading along the shore as well as numerous tropical birds for which this is the northernmost range. For a quieter scene, take the nature trail on the south side of the lake that leads to a shady grove frequented by both birds and deer. If you'd like to combine both bird sighting and scenery watching, try a pontoon-boat tour of the lake.

Patagonia Lake Open daily 4 a.m.–10 p.m. Entrance fee: $5/vehicle. Campsites: $10–$15/per night (no reservations). Pontoon-boat lake tours depart every Saturday at 9 a.m. Call 520-287-2791 to reserve seats. Drive southwest of Patagonia on AZ Hwy. 82 about seven miles. The turnoff to the lake is clearly marked. Turn west and drive four miles to the park entrance at 400 Patagonia Lake Road, Patagonia, AZ 85624. For further information, call 520-287-6965 or visit www.pr.state.az.us/parkhtml/patagonia.html.

Patagonia-Sonoita Creek Preserve Open Wed.-Sun., 7:30 a.m.-4 p.m. Docents lead nature walks every Saturday and Wednesday morning. Admission: adults $5, children under 16 free. The entry fee is good for seven days. From Patagonia, take 4th Avenue to Pennsylvania Avenue, then turn left and go 1¾ miles to the preserve. For further information, call 520-394-2400 or visit www.tncarizona.org/preserves/patagonia.asp. The community of Patagonia also maintains a website at www.patagoniaaz.com.

San Rafael Valley

South of Sonoita and Patagonia lies the San Rafael Valley, about 90,000 acres of rolling grasslands that takes its name from the original 1825 Mexican land grant, San Rafael de la Zanja. Most of the valley floor is privately owned ranch land, and the surrounding higher elevations are part of the Coronado National Forest. The southern boundary is the Mexican border. As the location of the headwaters of the Santa Cruz

River, the area is vital to the health of the watershed, and its moist areas are home to many endangered and sensitive species of plants. It is prime habitat for grassland birds including Cassin's and Botteri's sparrows in summer and longspurs and Baird's sparrow in winter. Bald eagles are occasionally seen in winter.

The land appears serene, but in the dwindling years of the 20th century it was the scene of cliff-hanging negotiations to keep it in its pristine state.

In 1997 the owners of the 22,000-acre San Rafael Ranch, the heart of the valley, needed to sell their property and faced the possibility that it would go to developers who would divide it up, forever changing the ecology of the area and closing off important wildlife corridors.

In a landmark deal that took several years to arrange, The Nature Conservancy bought the ranch and established permanent conservation easements

FISHING

WATER IS ALWAYS PRECIOUS IN THE DESERT, and when it comes in a quantity big enough to be called a lake, it is especially cherished. These fishing lakes also offer opportunities for camping in spectacular scenery. Remember, an Arizona fishing license is required for taking any aquatic wildlife. Visitors can purchase four-month nonresident licenses.

Fishing on Roper Lake.
LARRY LINDAHL

Cluff Ranch Ponds Formed by the damming of Ash Creek, these ponds are stocked with trout once a month by the Arizona State Game and Fish Department. You can also catch bass, catfish, crappie, and sunfish. The ponds are rimmed with cottonwoods and there are a few primitive campgrounds you can use at no charge. From U.S. Hwy. 70 in Pima, which is nine miles west of Safford, turn south on Main Street and go 1 1/2 miles. The road curves west and becomes Cottonwood Road. Continue another half mile, then turn south and go 4 1/2 miles. For further information, call 928-485-9430 or 520-628-5376.

Parker Canyon Lake This 132-acre body of water is a National Forest Recreation Site. You can catch rainbow trout, bass, sunfish, northern pike, and catfish. There's a boat ramp and a 64-space campground ($10/space nightly). The lake is located 28 miles south of Sonoita

and west of the Huachuca Mountains on AZ Hwy. 83. For further information, call 520-455-5847 or visit www.fs.fed.us/r3/coronado/svrd/parker.

Patagonia Lake This state park lake is filled with bass, crappie, bluegill, sunfish, and flathead and channel catfish. A dam across Sonoita Creek created the 265-acre lake. You can rent a boat or bring your own, or cool off at the swimming beach. Entrance fee: $5/vehicle. Camping fee: $10–$15. Drive seven miles west of Patagonia on AZ Hwy. 82. For further information, call 520-287-6063 or go to www.pr.state.az.us/parkhtml/patagonia.html.

Riggs Flat Lake This small lake is set among alpine forests and meadows in the Pinaleño Mountains and is well stocked with trout. From Safford, travel south on U.S. Hwy. 191 approximately nine miles to AZ Hwy. 366 (Swift Trail). Turn right and follow the road to the top of Mount Graham. The paved road becomes rough dirt at Columbine Ranger Station. For more information, call 928-428-4150 or visit www.fs.fed.us/r3/coronado/so/wildlife/fishing/lakes/lake03.

Roper Lake and Dankworth Ponds The Arizona State Parks Department administers these recreational areas. The 32-acre Roper Lake contains catfish, bluegill, large-mouth bass, and trout. You can use a boat with a trolling motor. Camping sites have hookups ($10–$17), and there's a dump station and showers. After a swim at the beach, relax in a natural hot tub fed from a mineral spring. The park is located off U.S. Hwy. 191 six miles south of Safford. Dankworth Pond lies three miles south of Roper Lake. For further information, call 928-428-6760 or visit www.pr.state.az.us/parkhtml/roper.html.

Felt-tip, ball-point, and pencil drawing by
Sam Donaldson of the Empire Ranch.

on the entire parcel to restrict subdivision and other incompatible uses. It then sold part to a private rancher and the rest to the State of Arizona for a new park, which is under development. The state park land includes the Territorial-style 1898 ranch house, which, along with the rolling grasslands, was used in at least two movies, including John Wayne and Maureen O'Hara's *McLintock*. The house will eventually be open for tours as part of the interpretive area. The Nature Conservancy also has negotiated a conservation easement on another, smaller ranch in the valley. If similar arrangements can be made for other San Rafael properties as they come on the market, environmentalists expect that the character of the valley can be maintained.

Grasses and blue skies prevail in the San Rafael Valley.
MILLS TANDY

Cattails and cottonwood trees at dawn, San Pedro
National Conservation Area.   JACK DYKINGA

Boomtowns & a River

3. MOTHER NATURE WAS GENEROUS when she created the landscape that visitors see in the San Pedro River Valley: a narrow river looping under towering cottonwoods and through cool, wooded mountains, and deep canyons harboring jewel-toned tropical birds. But it was the hidden treasures—silver, gold, copper, and semiprecious stones—that opened the door to the mining boom, the raucous extravaganza of wealth that spawned the most American of myths: the Old West drama of gamblers and lawmen and crooked cowboys.

When silver was discovered near Tombstone, the news spread like a grass fire, and the rush was on. As soon as new mines were located, towns sprang up beside them: Pearce, Fairbank, Gouge-Eye, Contention City, Total Wreck.

But the mines played out, the people moved on, and the desert reclaimed the town sites, with tumbleweeds piling up against any walls left standing. Today travelers come not for the mineral wealth but to enjoy the rich ecology of the San Pedro River Valley. The stands of cottonwood and willow and the mesquite bosques shelter so many plants and animals that the valley is now a national conservation area designated by The Nature Conservancy as one of the northern hemisphere's "Last Great Places."

In the Footsteps of Coronado

It was February 1540 when the Spanish explorer Francisco Vásquez de Coronado entered what is now the United States, leading an expedition north along the San Pedro River. In the first major European exploration of the American Southwest, Coronado

A 1903 faro game at the Orient Saloon on Main Street, Bisbee.

had been sent from New Spain (now Mexico) to find the seven great cities of gold rumored to exist in the north. He also hoped to spread the word of God for the Roman Catholic Church and expand the Spanish territory. Unaware that they were riding over a fortune in buried silver and gold ore near today's Bisbee and

Tombstone, Coronado and his party made their way to what is now Zuni in northern New Mexico, only to discover that the cities were made of adobe—nothing other than dried mud.

You can learn the story of this early Spanish expedition at the Coronado National Memorial a few miles from the spot where many scholars believe Coronado must have crossed. On weekends, rangers give history and nature programs. A steep ¾-mile climb above the museum brings you to a 600-foot-long cavern that visitors can explore. Signs along the trail post quotations from members of Coronado's party. You must have two flashlights for each person to get the ranger's permission to enter the cave.

Coronado National Memorial The visitor center is open daily 8 a.m.–5 p.m., except Thanksgiving and Christmas. The picnic area is open dawn to dusk, located off AZ Hwy. 92 about 12 miles south of Sierra Vista and 20 miles west of Bisbee. The turnoff to Coronado Memorial Drive is clearly marked, and the visitor center is six miles south of AZ Hwy. 92. For more information, call 520-366-5515 or visit www.nps.gov/coro.

Fort Huachuca & Sierra Vista

Established in 1877 as a remote outpost to protect the border with Mexico and guard against Apache attacks, Fort Huachuca is now at the forefront of America's defense as a headquarters for Army intelligence training. In the U.S. Army Intelligence Museum here, you can learn how surveillance and reconnaissance have developed over the last century, from troopers sent out on horseback to the latest surreptitious electronic listening devices.

To step back into the 19th century, visit the Fort Huachuca Historical Museum. Displays prompt your imagination with mannequins dressed in period costume. One exhibit gives the history of the famed

Montezuma Peak and Huachuca Mountains, from Coronado National Memorial. LAURENCE PARENT

Pages 34-35 Ascending a fixed rope in Dry Canyon, Whetstone and Dragoon Mountains in distance. ANDREW KORNYLAK

Buffalo Soldiers, a unit of African-Americans who fought the Indians and rode with Brig. Gen. John J. Pershing to Mexico in 1916. During World War II, the fort was the only infantry training post for blacks.

You can also drive by the original officers' homes arrayed around the parade field at the center of the Old Post. In December many of the officers' homes are decorated for Christmas and opened to the public.

Also worth a stop is the park-like post cemetery that is the final resting place for early-day cavalrymen, pioneers, Apache scouts, teamsters, and any unknown bodies the early soldiers found on the desert.

Beyond the developed area of the fort is a popular hiking spot called Garden Canyon. At one time fresh vegetables were grown there for the soldiers. At higher elevations you may find red and black rock art that was created by Indians around A.D. 1200.

Fort Huachuca is on the edge of the up-and-coming town of Sierra Vista. The name is Spanish for "mountain view," referring to the picturesque Huachuca Mountains. Surrounded by attractions and plentifully supplied with restaurants, accommodations, and shopping, Sierra Vista can be a visitor's base for other explorations. Incorporated in 1956, Sierra Vista is a celebration of the modern rather than the old. It has at least one historic site, however, one that may become more celebrated with time: The McDonald's on Fry Boulevard opened the first drive-though window of that popular chain in January 1975.

Old-timers reminisce outside
the Crystal Palace in Tombstone.
LARRY LINDAHL

Fort Huachuca The Fort Huachuca Historical Museum is open 9 a.m.–4 p.m. weekdays and 1–4 p.m. weekends. The U.S. Army Intelligence Museum is open 10 a.m.–2 p.m. Mon., Wed., and Fri. Both museums are closed on major holidays. Civilian visitors must have driver's license, vehicle registration, and proof of insurance to enter the post. Admission is free, donation suggested. The post may close for military alerts, so call 520-533-5736 before going. The museum's web address is huachuca-www.army .mil/history/museum.htm.

Tombstone

Every decade or so brings a new Tombstone movie concentrating on what we know as the Gunfight at the OK Corral. That battle was only a few seconds long, but it has come to overshadow the complex history of this quintessential Old West town.

The story began in 1877 when a prospector named Ed Schieffelin was combing Southeastern Arizona looking for a silver strike. Fort Huachuca soldiers told him he was not only wasting his time but would probably meet his maker at the hands of the Apaches. "The only thing you'll find there is your tombstone," they said. In fact, Schieffelin did find silver, and in honor of his doubting friends named his first two claims Graveyard and Tombstone. Then he found much richer claims of almost pure silver that he named the Lucky Cuss and Toughnut.

Word spread fast. Prospectors, financiers, miners, gamblers, and business folk came by stage, horseback, and foot to claim a piece of the bonanza. Saloons and gambling parlors lined the streets and were open around the clock. Scams were rife. A handful of nearby ranchers—accustomed to appropriating any cattle they found and selling them as quickly as possible—added to the political and economic stew. By 1880, the town of Tombstone had 10,000 inhabitants aligned in several well-armed factions.

One of the festering disagreements came to a head on an October afternoon in 1881 when the Earp brothers—Wyatt, Morgan, and Virgil (the town marshal), and their buddy Doc Holliday—shot it out with rancher-outlaws from the McLaury and Clanton families. The incident might have faded into history, but a biographer caught up with Wyatt years later and wrote his side of the story, and it caught the public imagination. You can see a reenactment of the shoot-out within yards of where it occurred and visit the Crystal Palace saloon where the Earps and their friends gambled and plotted.

Other attractions that have managed to survive from the good old days are the office of the newspaper, *The Tombstone Epitaph;* Boothill Cemetery, which holds honest-to-goodness outlaw graves; and the Bird Cage Theatre. The Bird Cage is a bit dusty and tattered but genuine. A *New York Times* article in 1882 called it the "wildest wickedest nightspot between Basin Street and the Barbary Coast." It was locked up when the town closed down in 1889 after

Tombstone Courthouse State Historic Park's museum includes displays on the area's ranching, mining, and gambling. BERNADETTE HEATH

the mines flooded, and the doors were not opened again until 1934. Also interesting is the Rose Tree Museum, home of the world's largest rosebush. Planted by a homesick English bride in 1885, the Lady Banksia rose covers at least 8,000 square feet and blooms between mid-March and mid-April.

For a comprehensive history of the town, visit the historic red brick Tombstone Courthouse, now a state park. You'll see the courtroom where justice was dealt and the guilty sent to the gallows outside, learn about the development of the mines and business interests, and meet the colorful citizens, both honorable and shady.

Tombstone presents Western-theme events every month, but the granddaddy of them all is Helldorado Days in mid-October with hourly gunfights, lawmen, and loose ladies parading the boardwalk, and stagecoaches rumbling down the street.

It took the Tombstone-Bisbee Stage a full day to go the 24 miles from Bisbee to Tombstone—and another day back.

Tombstone For general information, visit www.tombstone.org.

OK Corral Open daily 9 a.m.–5 p.m., gunfight daily at 2 p.m. Admission: adults $2.50, children under 6 free. Find information at www.ok-corral.com.

Bird Cage Theatre Museum Open daily 8 a.m.–6 p.m. Admission: adults $5, children 8–18 $4, children 7 and under free.

Tombstone Courthouse State Historic Park
Open daily 8 a.m.–5 p.m. Admission: adults $2.50, children 7–13 $1, children 6 and under free. 219 Toughnut St., Tombstone, AZ 85638. For further information, call 520-457-3311 or visit www.pr.state.az.us/parkhtml/tombstone.html.

Rose Tree Museum Open daily 9 a.m.–5 p.m. Admission: adults $3, children free with paid adult. 116 S. Fourth St., Tombstone, AZ 85638.

Boothill Cemetery Open daily 7:30 a.m.–6 p.m. Free admission.

The Shattuck Extension of the Phelps Dodge Lavender Pit mine, Bisbee.
RANDY PRENTICE

Bisbee

Mineral riches were found in the Bisbee area in the late 1870s, about the same time as in Tombstone. But because Bisbee's predominant ore was copper, the town developed differently and lasted longer.

Across the nation, factories and homes were installing electricity and needed copper wire in huge quantities. Experienced miners from Europe drilled, blasted, and mucked 2,000 miles of tunnels to get to the rich ore in the Copper Queen Mine. Miners were also extracting ore from an open pit. By 1900 Bisbee was producing 3 million pounds of copper a month and had more than 20,000 inhabitants, making it one of the largest cities between St. Louis and San Francisco. It was also dirty. Smelting that much ore

in the narrow canyons of the Mule Mountains led to high levels of pollution, which proved fatal to many native plants and was seriously unhealthful for the people as well. Eventually, the smelters were moved south to the new town of Douglas.

Bisbee miners and entrepreneurs built houses wherever they could. There is hardly any flat land for home sites, so the miners crammed their cabins together on the steep hillsides and then climbed hundreds of steps to get home to bed at the end of a long shift. Life in the canyons was not all work, however. Bisbee residents did their share of hell-raising, enough to support 47 saloons along Brewery Gulch.

The Bisbee mines continued to produce economically acceptable amounts of copper for decades. In addition to copper ore of various concentrations, there were also semiprecious stones: pure blue turquoise and green malachite, both formed when copper interacts with other substances.

When the mines finally closed in 1976, the residents of Bisbee knew they had to reinvent the town or lock their doors and move away. Real estate prices plunged, and the town became attractive to artists, who appreciated the turn-of-the-century architecture and the pleasant year-round climate. The retired miners who remained in the area were suspicious of new residents who had longer hair, colorful clothing, and counterculture ways, but as the years have passed, both the old-timers and the new residents who could get along with their neighbors have stayed, and others have drifted off.

Today Bisbee offers visitors a mixture of historical sites and information spiced with arts and antique shopping, athletic events, and quirky it-could-only-happen-here celebrations. You can learn about Bisbee's colorful past at the Mining and Historical Museum, an affiliate of the Smithsonian, then see the mines for yourself with a bus ride through the Lavender Pit, once the world's largest open-pit mine, or an underground tour of the Copper Queen led by retired miners.

A pleasant way to spend a day is just exploring the twisting streets of the town, popping into shops and galleries. Visit the Chamber of Commerce for a free illustrated guide to a walking tour of all the historic buildings. The restored Copper Queen Hotel in the middle of town is a must for visitors, as is the Muheim House, a restored Queen Anne home, where you'll learn how Bisbee's well-off citizens lived a century ago. It's a bit of a climb, but worth it, and you'll feel better about stopping in at the fudge shop later. If you don't want to walk, you can take the Bisbee Trolley Car that goes through town and out to nearby Warren, where the upper crust lived in mansions.

A rewarding side trip is a visit just south of town to the Arizona Cactus & Botanical Garden, where you can see more than 800 varieties of high desert plant life in the botanical garden and catch a class on landscaping with desert plants.

Annual Bisbee events include a challenging bicycle race through the steep hills called La Vuelta de Bisbee in April; the stair climb in October, during which participants race for five kilometers including 1,034 stairs; and the Brewery Gulch Days on Labor Day Weekend, when you never know what shenanigans to expect but can count on fun.

Bisbee For general information, visit www.bisbeearizona.com.

Queen Mine Tour Open daily. Reservations suggested. Admission: adults $10, children 7–9 $3.50, children 3–6 $2, kids under 3 free. Group rates are available. The mine tour building is immediately south of Old Bisbee's business district, off the US Hwy. 80 interchange. For further information, call toll-free 866-432-2071.

Surface Mines and Historic District Van Tour Operates daily. Admission: $7, children under 3 free.

Trolley Tour Operates daily except Wednesday. Admission: adults $10, children $7. 81 Main St. For further information, call 520-432-7020 or visit www.bisbeetrolley.com.

Moon over Douglas, oil painting by Alysa Bennett of the 99 Bar Ranch, Douglas.

Mining and Historical Museum Open daily 10 a.m.–4 p.m. except Christmas. Admission: adults $4, children 3–16 $1. 5 Copper Queen Plaza. For further information, call 520-432-7071 or visit www.bisbeemuseum.org.

Muheim House Open Fri.–Tues., 10 a.m.–4 p.m.; closed Christmas. Admission: adults $2, children under 16 free. 207 Youngblood Hill. For further information, call 520-432-7698 or drop by www.bisbeemuseum.org/muheim_house.htm.

Arizona Cactus & Botanical Garden Open daily, sunrise to sunset. Free guided tours. 8 South Cactus Lane. For further information, call 520-432-7040 or visit www.arizonacactus.com.

Benson

The history of the small town of Benson is tied to transportation. In the late 1800s, when travelers made the grueling, dusty cross-country trip on the Butterfield Trail, one of the stops was a stage station just a mile north of present-day Benson. The trip from the West Coast became more comfortable when the Southern Pacific Railroad reached Benson in June of 1880. Travelers going to Tombstone or Bisbee arrived on the train and transferred to stagecoaches or wagons.

KARTCHNER CAVERNS

Randy Tufts and Gary Tenen, the discoverers of Kartchner Caverns.

AS YOU LEAVE AZ HWY. 90 and enter the long driveway to Kartchner Caverns State Park, you see nothing but the unremarkable foothills of the Whetstone Mountains, the same view that college students Randy Tufts and Gary Tenen saw back in 1967 when they took a day off to go looking for caves. They found a sinkhole, but it was tiny, and they didn't return to it until 1974. This time they squeezed in and were left speechless at what they saw—a living cave with two long rooms full of still-growing formations glowing under their headlamps with fantastic colors of blood red, deep purple, and shimmering orange. Looking back, they say they felt "like we were representing the human race," and sensed a daunting responsibility. They knew they had to keep the cave a secret to protect it, but after 3 ½ years they decided to tell the Kartchner family, the ranchers who owned the property. Together they held the secret for another 10 years, concerned that others would find the entrance and desecrate this exquisite natural wonder. Eventually, they entered into highly confidential negotiations with the State of Arizona to turn the area into a state park.

Knowing that the cave took 330 million years to evolve and could have been ruined in a few months, the developers took care to ensure that the seven-acre cave would remain pristine. Over the years, the state committed $30 million to its development, and the staff takes seriously its charge of protecting this natural wonder. No more than 500 people a day are allowed in. On carefully monitored tours, visitors see rooms as big as football fields, some with formations as thin as soda straws dangling from the ceiling and others that look like giant draperies and multicolored towers, all of them formed by water dripping from the ceiling and carrying dissolved limestone. When you visit, plan to arrive at least an hour before your scheduled tour to watch the video in the Discovery Center and learn how the cave was formed.

Kartchner Caverns State Park Open daily 7:30 a.m.–6 p.m. Closed Christmas. Admission: $10/car. Cave tours: adults $14, children 7–13 $6. Campsites with hookups: $15/night. You must make reservations for the cave tours a month or more in advance. For reservations and further information, call 520-586-2283 or visit www.pr.state.az.us/parkhtml/kartchner.html.

SINGING WIND BOOKSTORE

WHEN EVERYWHERE ELSE IN THE COUNTRY shops are clamoring for mall space or prime downtown real estate, the most popular bookstore in Southeastern Arizona is found down a dirt road on a working ranch outside of Benson. Loyal customers do not seem to be bothered by the fact that you must open and close a cattle gate to get to the bookstore.

Win Bundy, the owner, is a rancher and former librarian. She opened her bookstore in 1974, first specializing in a few shelves of books relating to the Southwest. Now her collection has expanded to include every subject and taken over half her house. Busloads of people come by on tour. Bundy is happy to see them so long as somebody closes the gate to keep her livestock at home.

Every year on the Sunday before Thanksgiving, Bundy throws a festival. She lines up a band or two and invites authors to read and sign their latest works. Everybody is invited. And she even provides valet parking. As her loyal customers have learned over the

Ocotillo, oil painting by Alysa Bennett of the 99 Bar Ranch, Douglas.

years, Singing Wind bookstore is worth a special trip. Win Bundy knows exactly the books you'll love.

Singing Wind Bookstore Take exit 304 off I-10 in Benson. Go north about 2 1/4 miles to Singing Wind Road, turn right, and drive 1/2 mile to the shop. Open daily 9 a.m.–5 p.m. except major holidays. Call 520-586-2425 for more information.

After the decline of mining, Benson became a center for agriculture and ranching. The opening of nearby Kartchner Caverns in 2001 has provided an enormous economic stimulus to the area. Although Benson itself has few tourist attractions, it welcomes visitors at the San Pedro Valley Arts and Historical Society Museum, which occupies a small former grocery store and houses an eclectic mix of artifacts. Of particular interest is a sampling of early styles of barbed wire by the back door. The creative variety of such a utilitarian item is an eloquent testimony to what we have lost in the modern trend toward standardization.

San Pedro Arts and Historical Society Open May–July and Sept., Tues.–Sat. 10 a.m.–2 p.m.; and Oct.–Apr., Tues.–Fri. 10 a.m.–4 p.m. and Sat. 10 a.m.–2 p.m. Free admission. 180 South San Pedro at the intersection of 5th Street and San Pedro. For further information, call 520-586-3070.

A River Recovered

As the 19th century came to a close, the San Pedro Valley was an ecological disaster. The mining years had been hard on the land. Before electricity, the mines relied on cordwood to run the pumps and mills, denuding the nearby mountains of anything that could burn. This meant that during heavy summer rains, there were no plants to slow the rush of water down the slopes, and it scoured the canyons and cut deep arroyos on the plains. Ranchers, in their eagerness to feed the miners and export cattle, had overstocked the land, and the cattle ate what grass there was on the plains to stubble.

Then, in 1885, a series of drought years began. Streams and springs dried up. Thousands of head of cattle milled around the few remaining watercourses, particularly the San Pedro River, and ate and trampled the plants that could keep the ecosystem healthy. The years of 1891 and 1892 were the worst, when almost no summer rain fell. It was devastating for the ranchers.

A gallery forest of Fremont cottonwood trees along the meandering San Pedro River at dawn.   JACK DYKINGA

Estimates put the Southeastern Arizona cattle population in those years at more than 377,000, and half to three-quarters of the animals died.

After that, stock raising changed. Ranchers developed water sources through wells, windmills, and stock tanks and began to concentrate on quality cattle rather than sheer quantity.

Fortunately, if not pushed too far, some natural processes can begin to recover once the exploitation ceases. By the mid-1970s, the San Pedro River—a green ribbon through the usually buff-colored landscape—was gaining interest as a wildlife preserve. Ecologists who had traced the San Pedro River back to its origins found that it rose in the foothills of the Sierra Madre Occidental nearly 100 miles into Mexico. As it flows north of the border for about 140 miles, it is joined by the rainfall and melted snow from a watershed that includes 11 Southeastern Arizona mountain ranges until, near Globe, it merges with the Gila River.

Bird-watchers discovered long ago that the river is a migratory path for birds. The cottonwood-willow forests along the water produce more insects than any other forest type in the region, making it a hospitable flyway for birds, with plenty of food and trees and bushes to provide comfortable nighttime cover. By 1978, the area was being considered for purchase by the National Land Heritage Program.

Then, in a move that left conservationists gasping, two large tracts of land were sold to a land developer who had plans to put in a big housing development. It could have dealt the final blow to this valuable ecological space, but over the next 10 years the Bureau of Land Management managed to put together a complicated land deal in which the developer swapped his 43,000 acres of San Pedro land for a similar-sized parcel west of Phoenix.

In the fall of 1988, Congress created the San Pedro Riparian National Conservation Area. All motor vehicles and mining are banned, and cattle grazing has been halted temporarily. Beavers have been reintroduced, and they are once again building dams, forming marshy areas along the river and slowing the flow of the water. The river is teeming with life—100 different kinds of butterflies, 83 different mammals, turtles, 47 varieties of reptiles and amphibians. For all its remoteness, this can be a noisy place. Birds twitter and sing, frogs croak, and at night coyotes sing to the stars.

Male vermilion flycatcher.
TOM VEZO

Visitors are welcome to hike, bird-watch, or sit under a cottonwood and contemplate. A well-developed trail system runs the length of the conservation area. You can travel along the San Pedro on horseback, on mountain bike, or on foot and, with a permit from the BLM, camp overnight.

The information headquarters for the conservation area is San Pedro House on AZ Hwy. 90 near the river. Members of the support group Friends of the San Pedro frequently lead hikes through the area. Among them is one to Murray Springs, a place where about 13,000 years ago people of the Clovis culture killed a mammoth, a bison, and some other animals and apparently had a barbecue. Interpretive signs help you understand the site. You can also get there by yourself by taking the trail from San Pedro House or drive in one mile on Moson Road, which exits north off AZ Hwy. 90. Leave your car at the parking lot and follow the trail.

The protection of the San Pedro River has sparked controversy. Competing interests want access to the

A HAVEN FOR BIRD-WATCHERS

Male elegant trogon.
C. ALLAN MORGAN

IF BIRD-WATCHING IS YOUR PASSION, Southeastern Arizona is your spot. Some birds live here all year long, others come for only the summer or winter, and still others just pass through to or from tropical Mexico. You'll find species that frequent the grasslands, or prefer the deep shady canyons or the pine forests, or seek out the wetlands and shallow lakes. If you search in mountain canyons between April and September, you might see the large and brilliantly colored elegant trogon, a tropical bird that comes across the border into the sycamores of Madera Canyon, Cave Creek Canyon, and a few other spots.

In 1995 the American Bird Conservancy named the San Pedro Riparian National Conservation Area as the first "Globally Important Bird Area" in North America. About 400 species of birds—half the number of species in the entire United States—have been spotted in the San Pedro Valley, and 105 of these species breed there. There are so many birds that you don't have to be an expert to see a wide enough variety to make it fun.

The best place to begin your exploration of the San Pedro River area is San Pedro House on the west side of the river along AZ Hwy. 90. In the shop, you'll find books to help you identify what you see, a schedule of guided walks, and a trail map. Longer trails lead up and down the river and a 1½ -mile-long loop path takes you along the river to a small pond. Along the way, rustic benches offer the opportunity for you to stop and let the birds come to you. And come they will: tiny red vermilion flycatchers, ladder-back woodpeckers, and belted and green kingfishers. You'll also hear their cheeps, trills, titters, coos, and quacks rising above the soft burble of the flowing water.

The Ramsey Canyon Preserve south of Sierra Vista is known as the hummingbird capital of the United States, a place where birders glimpse 14 different species every year. Owned by The Nature Conservancy, the 300-acre property runs along Ramsey Creek. You are apt to see magnificent, blue-throated, white-eared, and even the rare berylline hummingbirds. The magnificent hummingbird sports arresting iridescent feathers, and it and the blue-throated are almost twice the size of the normally tiny birds.

Because the Ramsey Canyon area embraces everything from semi-desert grassland to pine forest, it is also home to more than 150 other bird species, including the sulphur-bellied flycatcher and the painted redstart in the summer and the bridled titmouse and Arizona woodpecker year-round. A naturalist leads walks at 9 a.m. every Tuesday, Thursday, and Saturday from March through October.

In order to control the human impact on the area, parking is limited to 23 spaces on a first-come, first-served basis. If you find the lot full, consider backtracking to the Brown Canyon Trail, which leads off the north side of Ramsey Canyon Road where the grasslands meet the oaks. It's about 1½ miles from AZ Hwy. 92. You'll find many of the same birds as in Ramsey Canyon, and in the late-summer rainy season you'll be able to enjoy spotting up to 50 different kinds of butterflies.

If only hummingbirds will do, an alternate area nearby is Beatty's Miller Canyon Guest Ranch and Orchard, 2173 E. Miller Canyon Rd., where you will see many hummingbirds at a time at their public feeder station. Each rental cabin has its own feeders. To visit this area, park in the Forest Service lot; do not block the Beattys' driveway, and respect the privacy of the residents. Miller Canyon Road turns to the west seven miles south of Sierra Vista. Call 520-378-2728 for more information.

A major winter event for bird-watchers is the arrival of the sandhill cranes. About 12,000 of these huge birds arrive in the Sulphur Springs Valley each October. They congregate in and around the Willcox Playa and Whitewater Draw Wildlife Area. At dawn they lift off together and fly several miles to feed on the leftover corn in the nearby harvested fields, then they go to another area to loaf for the day, returning to the fields in late afternoon for dinner. About sunset, they go back to the wetlands where they stand in the shallow water all night. The Arizona Electric Power Cooperative (AEPCO) Apache Generating Station between Cochise and Sunsites on U.S. Hwy. 191 has built a viewing platform on the edge of the wetlands, a convenient spot to see the cranes leave in the morning and return in the evening. You can get to the Whitewater Draw by traveling along U.S. Hwy. 191 between Sunizona and Elfrida and taking Rucker Canyon Road to the east or Gleeson Road to the west, then going south on Coffman Road.

With their wingspan of six or seven feet, sandhill cranes are easy to see as flocks circle in the sky during their regular daily movements. You can also hear their loud rattling "garrooo, garrooo" up to a mile away. Although they stand about 3 1/2 feet tall, you need binoculars to get a good look because they won't let you get close. You may be lucky enough to see a rare whooping crane raised by sandhill cranes as part of the federal endangered species program. By late February, the sandhill cranes are beginning to return to their nesting areas in Idaho, Wyoming, Montana, and Utah.

Other important bird-viewing areas are Patagonia-Sonoita Creek Preserve, Patagonia Lake State Park, Madera Canyon, the San Rafael grasslands, Chiricahua National Monument and Cave Creek Canyon near Portal, and the Empire Ranch in the Las Cienegas Conservation Area, all discussed elsewhere in this book.

Ramsey Canyon Preserve Open Mar.–Oct. 8 a.m.–5 p.m., Nov.–Feb. 9 a.m.–5 p.m. Closed Thanksgiving, Christmas, and New Year's Day. Admission: adults $5, children under 16 free. Take AZ Hwy. 92 about six miles south of Sierra Vista, turn right on Ramsey Canyon Road, and drive four miles to the end. Parking is limited to 23 vehicles. For further information, call 520-378-2785 or visit www.tncarizona.org/preserves/ramsey.asp.

The Southeastern Arizona Bird Observatory
This group sponsors the Southwest Wings Birding and Nature Festival every August. It includes three days of guided field trips to top birding areas. The observatory also offers weekend workshops and guided walks throughout the year. For further information, contact the Southeastern Arizona Bird Observatory at 520-432-1388 or www.sabo.org.

Wings Over Willcox This three-day festival is held every third week of January in Willcox. It celebrates sandhill cranes but also includes hawk stalks, sparrow seeks, and geology and photography tours. Wings over Willcox, c/o Willcox Chamber of Commerce and Agriculture, 1500 North Circle I Rd., Willcox, AZ 85643. For further information, call toll-free 800-200-2272 or visit www.wingsoverwillcox.com.

water and the plants it nourishes. Fort Huachuca and Sierra Vista are expanding, and new households mean more water use and demands on resources that feed the river. Ranchers are irked at losing rich grazing lands and maintain that well-managed cattle raising is beneficial to the ecosystem.

The San Pedro is a small river, sometimes just a trickle, sometimes retreating underground, leaving only damp sand on the surface, but it is the last free-flowing river in the Southwest. Now that Mother Nature has some partners in watching over this ecological gem, it has a much-improved chance of survival.

Ghost Towns

The years between 1880 and 1940 saw the quick flourishing and even quicker decay of dozens of small mining towns in Southeastern Arizona. A valuable resource such as silver or gold would be discovered, people would rush in, and houses, stores, and municipal buildings would go up. Then in a few years the mine would be exhausted or there would be a flood or a fire or the price for the ore would drop. People left town as quickly as they came, hoping to get to the next boomtown while they could still profit.

Many ghost town sites consist of nothing but a crumbling adobe wall and a few sticks of wood. Some town sites are privately owned and posted with "No Trespassing" signs.

A few ghost towns, however, are easy to get to and offer buildings to explore. Passenger cars can easily handle the graded gravel roads leading to these sites. Be extremely cautious near old mines as they are unstable and you could easily be injured if you tumbled into an uncovered shaft. Don't go down the shaft.

Presidio Santa Cruz de Terrenate This is a ghost town so old even the ghosts have fled. Terrenate was one of the most remote presidios established by New Spain. When the location was chosen in late 1775, 12-foot-high adobe walls were built to begin the enclosure, but in July 1776 Apaches

Pearce ghost town.
J. KEITH SCHREIBER

killed the commander and 29 soldiers, more than half the contingent. The presidio was re-staffed several times, but the Apaches were constantly on the attack. Finally, in 1780, the Spanish conceded that the outpost was indefensible and abandoned it. Although what remains is little more than melting adobe walls, it is the most intact example of what was formerly a string of similar fortresses.

To get there from AZ Hwy. 82, turn north on Iron Horse Ranch Road at mile marker 60, which is on the west side of the San Pedro just beyond Fairbank. Drive about two miles from the parking area. A mile-long trail leads to the site, where you will find interpretive signs. Remember how old these ruins are and treat them gently.

Kentucky Camp Located in the eastern foothills of the Santa Rita Mountains near the Greaterville gold-mining district, Kentucky Camp was established in 1900 as the headquarters for the Santa Rita Water and Mining Company. The plan was to dam the water that flowed down the mountain from rain and melting snow and use it to wash out the gold, an operation that after a mere two years proved more costly than the value of the gold that was extracted.

To get to Kentucky Camp, turn off AZ Hwy. 83 (between I-10 and Sonoita) onto Gardner Canyon Road (Forest Service Road 92). After a mile, turn right, then go another five miles to Kentucky Camp. Park at the gated entrance and walk a quarter mile to the buildings.

Fairbank Fairbank was a railroad town and the closest the train came to Tombstone and Bisbee. The train took the ore out and brought in goods, including produce, fish, and oysters kept fresh with ice. Incorporated in 1881, the town had a population of nearly 15,000 at its peak and boasted a hotel, a school, restaurants, and a general store.

A quarter-mile walk from the old general store will bring you to the cemetery, located high on a hill to protect it from flooding by the San Pedro River. Most of the more than a hundred graves are marked only by piles of rock and weathered wooden crosses; a few are separated by rusted iron fences. Slightly more than a mile beyond the cemetery are the ruins of the Grand Central Mill site, where the silver ore was ground into powder.

Fairbank is next to AZ Hwy. 82, about six miles west of the U.S. Hwy. 80 junction.

Dos Cabezas The first Butterfield Stage stop to the west of Fort Bowie was Dos Cabezas (Two Heads), which refers to the two rounded peaks above the town. When gold was discovered in 1880, prospectors rushed in and stores, bars, and hotels were built to serve the miners and the ranchers who were also settling in the grass-rich valleys.

The gold deposits were soon exhausted, but then copper was discovered on the twin peaks. Copper mining requires capital, and it came in the form of the Mascot Copper Company. The operators sold stock, moved in heavy equipment, and brought in a railroad spur from Willcox. Soon the town could count 4,000 inhabitants. One thing that Mascot didn't do was mine much copper. It turned out that the company had been set up as a stock swindle from the beginning. When Wall Street took a dive in 1927, the company couldn't be saved, and the entire settlement faded away, with the best of the buildings being moved or dismantled for their lumber.

Today you can visit the Dos Cabezas cemetery and see a scattering of adobe buildings. A few people have moved in, enjoying the stillness.

Dos Cabezas is about 14 miles south of Willcox on U.S. Hwy. 191.

The Ghost Town Trail Three ghost towns have given the gravel road that cuts from Sunsites to Tombstone the name "Ghost Town Trail."

The northernmost town is Pearce, which boasts a handful of picturesque buildings and some actual live people. The town was founded in 1894 when a prospector named John Pearce stopped for lunch, found gold, and filed several claims for what became the Commonwealth Mine. It produced more than $15 million in gold and is still prominent above the town. By 1919 the town had a population of 1,500, a school, businesses— even a movie theatre. The general store, now closed except for special events, was built in 1896 and is on the National Register of Historic Places.

The ruins of Fort Bowie.
LARRY LINDAHL

The old post office is now home to the owners of Old Pearce Pottery, open Friday through Sunday. In addition to visiting that store, you might want to browse in Utter Delight, a short walk south of the town's only crossroads, where the owner, Marcia Bothman, uses the milk from her six purebred goats to make soap in more than 40 scents. The small museum showcasing the history of soaps and classic advertisements will leave you chuckling and reminiscing.

About 12 miles south of Pearce lies Courtland, where the concrete walls of the former jail are the most prominent feature. Across the road and slightly north, a sidewalk fronting a row of building foundations is all that remains of the business district. This town was founded in 1909 and survived until 1942 with such urban amenities as a car dealer, a movie theatre, two newspapers, and an ice cream parlor. Less than a mile south of the jail the remains of two buildings can be seen from the highway. Drive off the highway on the dirt road just to the west, and at the bottom of the hill you'll find the foundation of another house hidden behind mesquite trees. On the

hills above, shelves of tailings indicate the entrances to a number of mines.

Follow the Ghost Town Trail south and slightly west, and you'll find Gleeson, the site of an old Indian turquoise mine. A post office opened in 1900 and was given the name of John Gleeson, who found a rich vein of copper there. In 1912, much of the town burned, and by 1939 it was declining. The last mine closed in 1953, although the remains of the big Shannon Mine still loom over the town it dominated. The saloon on the corner of the highway and the main street is locked tight and, with tumbleweeds piled near the front door, appears to be closed for good. The old jail across the highway looks similar to the one in Courtland. Along the highway to the east of town, you'll find the walls of the adobe hospital; to the west is the cemetery, with ornate headstones from the time when Gleeson really was somewhere.

Gammons Gulch There is a bit of fantasy about all ghost towns, but Gammons Gulch has more than most. The town is not old, but most of the 17 buildings have a long history. City father Jay Gammons

San Rafael Ranch cowboys, 1897.

Hayride at the San José Ranch near the border town of Naco.

has bought, scrounged, and transported Old West-era buildings from several states and collected them in an authentic-appearing ghost town in the middle of the desert north of Benson. To provide a period ambiance, Gammons replicated the width of boardwalks and the spacing of buildings in old towns. Along the way, he also found a mountain of historic old stuff. Among the relics that he occasionally rents out to decorate movie sets are a 1908 round icebox and an 1880s bellows.

Gammons Gulch is usually open Wednesday through Sunday. Call 520-212-2831 for hours and to make sure they'll be open. There is a modest admission charge. To get there, take the Pomerene Road exit off I-10. Follow it for 12 miles and turn off on East Rock Spring Road. You'll soon see the sign.

Ruins of the cavalry barracks of Fort Bowie, in active use
from 1862 to 1894 during the time of the Apache conflicts.
GEORGE H. H. HUEY

Apaches & Hoodoos

Early marketing for WILLCOX

AMERIND Foundation

BILLIONS of STARS in the Black Night

4. THE EASTERN EDGE of Southern Arizona was Apache country. We remember that history today through many of the place names, such as the Chiricahua Mountains, Cochise Stronghold, and Apache Pass. When the United States acquired Southeastern Arizona through the Gadsden Purchase in 1854, the Chiricahua Apaches had already been raiding and fighting with the Spanish and Mexican settlers for more than two centuries.

The Apaches, who called themselves Chokonen, saw their hunting grounds and their water holes being taken over, and they fought fiercely to preserve their way of life. Since their attacks had driven off many an earlier rancher, the Apaches had no way of knowing that this time they faced a stronger foe and that the Americans would not back down when faced with their war parties.

Fort Bowie

There are places in Southeastern Arizona that remain just as lonely and remote today as they were in the middle of the 1800s. Fort Bowie is such a place.

Near there, the water from Apache Spring softly gurgles into a tiny pond banked by rocks in a shady glen. Such a pretty place to have been the scene of so much bloodshed! The Chiricahua Apaches frequently congregated near the reliable spring, a rare desert resource. The corridor between the Dos Cabezas and the Chiricahua mountains, called Apache Pass, is not far beyond the spring. When the route for the Butterfield Overland Stage was laid out in 1858 it went through the pass, and the spring suggested an ideal place to build the stagecoach station.

For a while, the operators of the stage station paid the Apaches to provide firewood for them, and periods of relative peace alternated with times of hostility.

A view from the Sugarloaf Mountain Trail in the Heart-of-Rocks area,
Chiricahua National Monument.   GEORGE H. H. HUEY

53

However, in 1861 when Cochise, the Apache leader, was falsely accused of a kidnapping, he and his followers declared war. In response, Fort Bowie was established just above the spring to protect travelers and white settlers. For the next 10 years, livestock raids and skirmishes occurred frequently until Cochise made peace with the U.S. government when he and his people were given a reservation in their homeland. The reservation included what we now call Cochise Stronghold, a stunningly beautiful area of towering granite cliffs and oak-shaded canyons in the Dragoon Mountains. Two years later, in 1874, Cochise died of natural causes and was buried in a still-secret grave deep inside this rugged natural fortress.

Today Cochise Stronghold is part of the Coronado National Forest and has a camping area under large oak trees as well as an easy nature walk and several more challenging hiking trails leading into the Dragoon Mountains. The huge boulders with their straight smooth faces have made Cochise Stronghold popular with rock climbers. If you walk around, you may see bodies inching their way up the sides of sheer cliffs.

A few years after Cochise died, the peace pact fell apart, and his people were moved to the San Carlos Reservation. Some Apaches, however, refused to live on the reservation. Among their leaders was Geronimo, an Apache medicine man. The United States, though, was not about to let the Apaches curtail the economic development of the Cochise Stronghold area. So after the Civil War, more than 5,000 men—a fifth of the U.S. Army—were sent to Southeastern Arizona to try to bring Geronimo under control.

Rock pinnacles at sunset, Rhyolite Canyon, Chiricahua Mountains.
SCOTT T. SMITH

The last Apaches, including Geronimo, surrendered in 1886, but Fort Bowie remained active for another eight years. Toward the end, the soldiers had a more comfortable life with a tennis court and an ice plant that allowed them to enjoy ice cream and cold beer. With more peaceful times at hand, the fort was abandoned in 1894.

A visit to Fort Bowie is a good way to gain insight into the life of a frontier soldier. As you walk the 1½-mile-long path from the parking area to the ruins of the fort, it is so quiet that you will hear the calls of birds, the wind rustling through the grass, and the sound of your own footsteps—a good indication of the degree of isolation the first soldiers encountered. Along the trail, you will pass the ruins of the Butterfield Station and what is left of the post graveyard. The remains of the soldiers have been moved to San Francisco, but there are still some civilian graves, including that of Geronimo's two-year-old son.

Once you arrive at the site, drop into the visitor center, where you can pick up maps and learn more about the fort. After you have explored the ruins, rather than retracing your route, you might consider returning via the Overlook Ridge Trail, which gives an interesting view of the fort area.

Fort Bowie The visitor center is open daily 8 a.m.–5 p.m. Closed Christmas. A 1½-mile trail leads from the parking area to the visitor center and the ruins. There are two routes to the Fort Bowie parking area. From Willcox, drive south 20 miles on AZ Hwy. 186. From the turnoff, drive eight miles on an unpaved road that leads to the parking area and trailhead. From the town of Bowie, drive south 13 miles on Apache Pass Road to the trailhead. For further information and to make arrangements for wheelchair access, call 520-847-2500 or visit www.nps.gov/fobo.

Willcox

The arrival of the railroad through Southeastern Arizona brought more consumer goods from the eastern markets and from California. In 1880, the Norton-Morgan General Store, the first major business in the town of Willcox, began selling food and manufactured items to the town's residents, to nearby ranchers, and to the Army forts. The store delivered large out-of-town orders by mule-drawn wagons, which were frequently attacked by Apaches.

Natchez and Geronimo at Fort Bowie, September 1886, just before their deportation to Florida. A. F. RANDALL

Once the Indians commandeered a load of white flour, and, when loading it on their ponies in haste, punctured the bags. Men sent to search for the stolen goods just followed the flour trail. In his peaceful periods, Geronimo was a customer of the store and regularly bought sugar there to take back to his people.

Today that store, in the same spot on Railroad Avenue, is called Willcox Commercial and houses a small museum with old photographs, examples of earlier merchandise, and other vintage items.

One of the Commercial's customers in the 1930s was a boy named Elvie Allen. Elvie—later known as Rex Allen—became a radio, movie, television, and recording star of the 1940s and 50s. Willcox was so proud of him that in 1951 it launched Rex Allen Days, which still offers a rodeo, parade, and other festivities on the first weekend in October. Until his death in 1999, Rex Allen always led the parade.

Toward the end of Allen's career the Smithsonian Institution asked him to donate his memorabilia. Rather than have his family pictures, silver saddle, and fringed, sequined costumes carefully wrapped and stored forever in a vault, he offered the collection to his Willcox friends. In turn, they developed the small Rex Allen Museum, which today includes the Willcox Cowboy Hall of Fame and some historic photographs.

Allen can be heard on a video describing the history of Willcox in a museum in the former Southern Pacific railroad station, which shares the space with City Hall. Across the street are a small antiques store and an espresso bar. The shop was formerly the dining room for two hotels that flanked it. For years, much of the town's business was done in this tiny building. By 1930, the railroad was shipping nearly 50,000 head of cattle a year. Many stock owners didn't trust the banks, so tall stacks of cash, deeds, and stock were traded at the tables while the ranchers had drinks and waited for the cattle train.

West of town is a natural phenomenon called the Willcox Playa, 50 square miles of grayish tan crust,

EARLY MARKETING
FOR **WILLCOX**

"THE CLIMATE IS SUPERB. World travelers concede it to surpass California, the Mediterranean section, and Northern Africa. Its altitude of 4,000 feet tempers the summer heat and the southern latitude eliminates winter.

"The dry pure atmosphere, blue skies, sunlight and moonlight, the southern breeze, the cool and refreshing nights, the absence of death-dealing tempest... combine to make conditions as nearly perfect as can be obtained."

— C.O. Anderson,
Willcox Board of Trade (1912),
as quoted in a display in the
Rex Allen Museum

Railroad Avenue, Willcox — the freighting center for Southeastern Arizona
after the arrival of the Southern Pacific Railroad in 1880.

the vestige of a lake that 30,000 years ago was 35 feet deep. Mirages frequently appear near the Willcox Playa, startling travelers who "see" miles and miles of shimmering lake. Archaeologists have found remnants of hundreds of early Native American campsites along its ancient beaches. During World War II, the Army used the playa as a bombing range, but these days the playa is being recognized as an important part of the ecology of the area. Late-summer monsoon rains and the gentler rains of winter usually leave sections of the lake bed covered with at least a shallow sheet of water, which, along with the grain fields to the east, attracts many bird species.

Willcox has become the produce capital of Southeastern Arizona. Farmers grow everything from apples to zucchini, and more than a dozen of them invite the public in to picnic under the trees and do their own picking if they wish.

Pages 58-59 Sandhill cranes in the
Whitewater Draw Wildlife Area. TOM VEZO

APACHES & HOODOOS   57

Warner Glenn on Snowy River and Kelly Glenn-Kimbro on Dollar, Malpai Ranch.
JAY DUSARD

Douglas

The Phelps Dodge mining operation established Douglas as a company town. By 1900, copper mining in nearby Bisbee had developed to the point where smelting the ore was causing serious pollution problems in the little canyon where the town is located. So 25 miles away, at a spot with abundant water and land, new smelters were set up, and the town was named after Dr. James Douglas, the president of Phelps Dodge. Dr. Douglas sent his son, James S. "Rawhide Jimmy" Douglas, to oversee the town's construction. Soon, more than half of Arizona's copper was being processed at the smelters there.

Commerce grew rapidly, and a busy town needs a place for visitors to stay. The five-story Gadsden Hotel was built in 1907. According to town legend, during the Mexican Revolution, Douglas residents would stand on the hotel roof for a good view of battles across the border. After the hotel burned down in 1927, it was rebuilt more resplendent than ever. In the lobby a wide white marble staircase rises to the base of a stained-glass mural by Tiffany guarded by a stuffed mountain lion. Marble columns topped with gold leaf stand among the comfortable lobby chairs.

While Rawhide Jimmy was seeing to the development of Douglas, he also built a lovely colonial revival home for his family. Today it is the Douglas/Williams House museum and the location of the Douglas Historical Society. There you can see the bedroom of young Lewis Douglas, who grew up to become the U.S. ambassador to England from 1947 to 1950.

It is easy to park in the lot at First and G Streets near the border and walk across the international line to the Mexican town of Agua Prieta (Dark Water). With around 100,000 residents, Agua Prieta is much larger than Douglas. The inhabitants are employed in ranching or by one of the 30 local manufacturing plants or *maquiladoras*. Here's a border town with shopping aimed at ordinary citizens rather than tourists. You'll find saddles, ropes, and cowboy boots in exotic leathers. Furniture stores carry merchandise appealing to the tastes of Mexicans, which can be formal and sometimes European in flavor. Appliance shops sell washing machines with old-fashioned hand wringers alongside the latest spin models.

Douglas/Williams House Museum Open 1–4 p.m. Tues.–Thurs. and Sat., except major holidays. Admission by donation. 1001 D Ave., Douglas, AZ 85607. For further information, call 520-364-7370 or visit www.vtc.net/~cinema/dwhouse.html.

"Chip," pencil drawing by Sam Donaldson of the Empire Ranch.

Historic Ranch Houses You Can Visit

Ranch houses were the nerve centers of big Arizona ranches—they served as residence and office for the ranchers, dining hall for the cowboys, social center for the neighbors, and veterinary clinic and sometimes nursery for the animals.

Visitors are welcome at two restored ranch houses, each giving an intriguing look at 19th-century life at a remote ranch.

Slaughter Ranch ˘ John Slaughter, a former Texas Ranger, bought the 65,000-acre San Bernardino Ranch, near Douglas, in 1884 when he was sheriff of Cochise County. The ranch was part of a large Mexican land grant and, at the time Slaughter bought it, spanned both sides of the still-unfenced international border. Slaughter himself was gone much of the time during his two terms as sheriff, so the running of the

Ranch house, outbuildings, and holding pond, John Slaughter Ranch near Douglas. BERNADETTE HEATH

busy operation fell largely to his wife, Viola. She looked after dozens and dozens of cowboys as well as her own mother, Slaughter's two children, several foster children, and a school for the youngsters. She also oversaw a Chinese cook, who baked 34 loaves of bread daily, had breakfast on the table at 4:30 every morning, and turned the ranch grapes into jam, wine, and brandy. Chinese farmers worked in gardens south of the house, growing vegetables for the ranch.

An important factor in the success of the San Bernardino Ranch was the ample water—a spring that still produces 60–100 gallons a minute and forms a small tree-shaded lake that is ideal for picnicking.

After the Slaughters sold the ranch and moved to town, the San Bernardino passed through several owners, was listed on the National Register of Historic Places, and was eventually sold to The Nature Conservancy in 1980. The Johnson Historical Museum of the Southwest took over the home site and 131 acres in 1982 and has restored and furnished the airy six-room adobe ranch house, as well as the icehouse, the commissary, and the wash house. Family photographs

Ranch house and hitching post, John Slaughter Ranch near Douglas. BERNADETTE HEATH

help to round out the story of life on this quintessential Southern Arizona ranch. The U.S. Fish and Wildlife Service operates the remaining land as the San Bernardino National Wildlife Refuge.

Slaughter Ranch Open Wed.–Sun., 10 a.m.–3 p.m. Closed Christmas and New Year's Day. Admission: adults $3, children under 14 free. 6153 Geronimo Trail. To visit, leave Douglas going east on 15th Street, which becomes Geronimo Trail. Drive 15 miles to

San Bernardino Valley & Peloncillo Mountains, Arizona.
JAY DUSARD

the well-marked white gate on the right. Visitors may picnic under the cottonwoods surrounding the pond. For further information, call 520-558-2474 or visit www.vtc.net/~sranch/.

Faraway Ranch Faraway Ranch, at the entrance to Chiricahua National Monument, was the product of the dreams of Emma Peterson, a young Swedish immigrant. In 1883 Emma was working as a housekeeper at a fort in New Mexico Territory when she met Neil Erickson, another Swede, who was an Indian-fighting cavalryman in the U.S. Army. They both moved separately to Arizona Territory—Emma to Fort Bowie and Neil to Fort McDowell and then Fort Huachuca. During their occasional meetings, they would ride out to picnic in beautiful Bonita Canyon, tucked into the eastern side of the Chiricahua Mountains. In 1886 Emma bought a

Woodcut, carved with pocketknife and inked with paints on hand on a grocery bag, by Sam Donaldson of the Empire Ranch.

two-room cabin in the canyon, and Neil filed a homestead claim on 160 acres.

The young couple married, moved into the cabin, bought cattle, and put in a big garden. But Neil hated farming and for years worked in Bisbee, seeing his growing family only occasionally because Emma refused to leave her ranch. In 1903, the federal government created the Chiricahua Forest Reserve, and Neil was appointed the first ranger, at last able to work close to home.

When Neil was transferred to the Flagstaff area, Emma went with him, leaving the operation of the ranch to their three grown children. Daughters Hildegarde and Lillian began taking in paying guests. Lillian's husband, Ed Riggs, loved the area and worked to have it designated a national monument and to lay out the trails for visitors. He and Lillian continued to give up to 30 guests at a time a healthful and entertaining experience of riding, hiking, swimming, and eating fresh fruits and vegetables from their garden.

After Lillian was widowed, she ran the ranch alone for many years, even through she had been blinded by a fall from a horse. Upon her death, the ranch became part of an expanded Chiricahua National Monument. The table in the dining room is set as if guests are still having drinks on the patio and will enter for dinner in a few minutes.

Faraway Ranch Open daily except Christmas. The Chiricahua National Monument entry fee of $6 includes Faraway Ranch. Ranger-guided tours leave from the visitors center at 2 p.m. Mon.–Fri. and 2 and 3:30 p.m. Sat.–Sun. From Willcox, take AZ Hwy. 186 for 32 miles south. The turnoff to the monument is clearly marked. From the turnoff, drive four miles to monument entrance. For further information, call 520-824-3560 or www.nps.gov/chir.

The Western Side of the Chiricahuas

Set between the Sulphur Springs Valley to the west and the San Simon Valley to the east, the Chiricahua Mountains rise to nearly 10,000 feet, harboring cool, piney woods, trickling streams, and canyons of eerie beauty. The mountain range is a detached section of the Coronado National Forest and stretches 40 miles from north to south and 20 miles across at the widest point. Because the slopes of this sky island encompass five distinct ecological zones, the area is home to a diverse collection of living things: 70 different mammals, 48 kinds of lizards and snakes, more than 300 species of birds, and 700 species of flowering plants.

During the summer, the mountains offer blessed relief from the heat of the desert, but the area attracts violent thunderstorms during July and August. Hikers should check the weather report to avoid getting caught in one of Arizona's classic downpours.

Roads that allow you to explore the Chiricahua backcountry in your vehicle are found mainly on the northern part of the range. Chiricahua National Monument is on the western slope, and the towns of Portal and Paradise and beautiful Cave Creek Canyon lie on the eastern slope. A sinuous, pitted road over Onion Saddle connects the east and west sides. It is only about 20 miles long, but leave at least two hours for the drive. The road is usually closed from November through March because of snow, and at other times you would be wise to attempt the trip only in perfect weather or in a high-clearance vehicle or on horseback. Most of the southern section of the Chiricahuas is roadless wilderness, although hikers can find miles of trails.

As a casual passerby at the base of the Chiricahua Mountains, you would never guess at the wonderland of lavender and orange spires and cliffs at their center, called the Heart of Rocks. To the Apaches,

A snowy view west from Massai Point, Chiricahua National Monument.
LAURENCE PARENT

Pool created by a waterfall in the South Fork of Cave Creek, near Portal. RANDY PRENTICE

Street, a long narrow passage hemmed in by sheer walls of volcanic rock. You will swear you have seen this in a movie, and it is easy to fantasize that at any minute either the Apaches or the cavalry will thunder through on their horses. If you hike the Echo Canyon Loop, go counter-clockwise and you will have the steeper part of the trail going down and a gentler return on Hailstone Trail.

The only place to spend the night at Chiricahua National Monument is the campground; if you don't want to camp, you will need to find a room in a nearby town or guest ranch.

this was the "Land of the Standing Up Rocks." The pinnacles, also called hoodoos, are composed of a material called rhyolite canyon tuff in alternating hard and soft layers. The rhyolite was once a solid block, almost 2,000 feet thick, but the shifts in the earth's crust have caused the material to crack and form smaller blocks. When the blocks of tuff were thrust upward, wind, dust, rain, and plant acids wore away the softer spots along the cracks, leaving the fascinating towers we see today.

Stop at the visitors center on the way in to Chiricahua National Monument and pick up a map. Although you can see a great deal from your car on a slow trip up Bonita Canyon Drive, the best way to experience the canyon is to get down into it, to be surrounded by the labyrinth of totems and spires and to hear the soft sigh of the wind. Every morning at 8:30, a shuttle leaves the visitors center and drops hikers off at one of two trailheads. Starting from Echo Canyon, you can take a mostly downhill hike of 4½ miles back to the visitors center. If you are more ambitious, you can take off from Massai Point and pass through the Heart of Rocks on the 7½-mile-long trail. Should you arrive later in the day, try a hike from the visitors center about three miles to the Heart of Rocks (and three miles back) or take the 3½-mile-long Echo Canyon Loop Trail. A particularly interesting feature in Echo Canyon is called Wall

Chiricahua National Monument Canyon and campground open daily. Entrance fee: $5/car. Camping: $8/night. Hiking shuttle: $2/person. From Willcox, take AZ Hwy. 186 for 32 miles south. The turnoff to the monument is clearly marked. From the turnoff, drive four miles to the monument entrance. For further information, call 520-824-3560 or visit www.nps.gov/chir.

Palmer's metal-mark butterfly. BERNADETTE HEATH

The Eastern Side of the Chiricahuas

The village of Portal is in fact the gateway to the eastern side of the Chiricahuas. Just beyond is Cave Creek Canyon, which has soaring pink-gold cliffs and domes, a softly trickling stream, wildflowers, grasses, and trees. It is a place of such stunning beauty that it is frequently referred to as "Arizona's Yosemite." For a

AMERIND FOUNDATION

THE AMERIND FOUNDATION MUSEUM is nestled into the boulder-strewn Texas Canyon near Dragoon. Devoted to American Indian archaeology, arts, history, and culture, the small museum with its softly lit displays of baskets and pottery is an elegant anomaly in a neighborhood of corrals and cactus. William S. Fulton, a Connecticut mining equipment magnate, was so intrigued by archaeology that he bought the ranch where the museum sits so that he could excavate the Indian ruins there. The foundation was established in 1937, and today employs top-notch professional archaeologists and is involved with critical investigations of the former inhabitants and cultures of Southern Arizona and other areas. After you have seen the Indian artifacts, be sure to visit the small art museum that displays the work of many prominent Western painters.

Cassin's kingbird.
TOM VEZO

The Amerind Foundation Museum Open daily 10 a.m.–4 p.m., Sept.–May; Wed.–Sun., June–Aug. Closed major holidays. Admission: adults $5, seniors $4, children 12–18 $3, children under 12 free. From I-10 at Texas Canyon, take Dragoon Road (exit 318) and drive one mile south to the Amerind entrance at 2100 N. Amerind Rd., Dragoon, AZ 85609. For further information, call 520-586-3666 or visit www.amerind.org.

good view, stop at the Vista Point parking lot about three miles beyond Portal and walk up to the overlook where you'll find a bench and scenery to make you draw in your breath. On the South Fork, hiking trails wind along the streambed, crossing and re-crossing it under the shade of walnut, sycamore, and cypress trees. In October, Rocky Mountain maples provide fall color, rare in this part of Arizona.

Native Americans lived near Cave Creek Canyon centuries in the past, but when Stephen Reed homesteaded it in 1878, the canyon was unknown and unnamed. He built a cabin, planted apple trees, had six children with his wife, Isabelle, then raised them himself after her horse dragged her to death.

The Reeds were not by themselves for long. In the late 19th century, the eastern side of the Chiricahua Mountains attracted prospectors and miners lured by the lead and silver ore. The town of Galeyville grew to 400 miners, businessmen, and outlaws between 1880 and 1882 and vanished just as quickly when the ore gave out. Some of the prospectors stayed in the area, looking for the next big strike, and by 1900 about a dozen men were camped along Turkey Creek. The next year a man named George Walker and a partner laid out a 20-acre town site. Walker then married a local girl and opened a store. Area residents had been calling the place Paradise, and when the

post office opened with Walker as postmaster, the name was formalized. The Chiricahua Mine was being developed, and soon there were 100 residents in town and another 200 nearby, enough to support a newspaper, a hotel, a restaurant, a bakery, 13 saloons, and a cemetery.

In 1908, however, the price of copper plummeted, the mine closed, and Paradise was on the downhill slide. For decades Paradise was nearly deserted, until in the winter of 1967 a group of young dreamers, the author of this book among them, moved onto a nearby ranch, hoping to establish homes and rebuild the town, making it a center for artists, writers, and New Age sensibilities. Power struggles and money woes put a stamp of reality on our fantasy, and we all eventually left, leaving the ghostly town site exactly as we had found it.

Others did drift in, however, and Paradise now has about a dozen full-time residents, with a few others who spend holidays and weekends there. Among the original buildings are the George Walker House, which has been restored and is now a bed-and- breakfast inn, and a small adobe building formerly attached to a hotel that burned down long ago. The 1½-acre cemetery is also still there and holds 118 graves behind an iron gate, including that of Walker himself.

Today, the eastern side of the Chiricahuas draws bird-watchers, hikers, and campers. In the summer, the shady canyons and higher-elevation camping areas offer cool respite for parched desert-dwellers.

For years both birds and bird-watchers alike have flocked to the back yard of the late ornithologist Sally Spofford. Although Dr. Spofford passed away in 2002, friends and neighbors have vowed to continue to welcome the 4,000–6,000 birders who turn up in her back yard every year. Human visitors will find benches, bird books, and checklists, but for the birds, the big attraction is food strung on clotheslines and stuffed in feeders. A 50-pound bag of sunflower seeds and 5,000 mealworms is only a three-week supply for the hungry birds. The feeding station attracts other animals as well. Skunks that stop by love dry dog food, while foxes prefer Fig Newtons and doughnut holes.

Five miles west of Portal, the American Museum of Natural History operates the Southwest Research Station to serve scientists who come from all over the world to study the diversity of plant and animal life and the geology of the Chiricahua Mountains. Researchers stay in simple cabins and eat communally in a dining room. A number of the scientists have found the area so pleasant that on retirement they have returned to live full-time. Often in the spring and fall and occasionally in the summer, the research station has room to accommodate visitors who have come for recreation rather than research.

At the Portal Store on the way to Paradise or Cave Creek Canyon, you can find trail maps, nature guides, and a good lunch. The Forest Service visitors center also has information, but it's open only seasonally.

Chiricahua Mountains, east side To get to Sally Spofford's famous birding site, drive about one mile west of Portal, turn left on Sierra Linda Ranch Road, and stay right until you see her sign. Do not call ahead. Guests are welcome. For information on Cave Creek Canyon and other forest areas, call the Douglas Ranger District at 520-364-3468 or try www.fs.fed.us/r3/coronado/douglas/index.

American Museum of Natural History Southwest Research Station From I-10, exit at US Hwy. 80, drive 25 miles south to AZ Hwy. 533, and turn west to Portal. The station is located five miles west of Portal in Cave Creek Canyon. Amateur naturalists and bird-watchers can be accommodated on a space-available basis, mostly in spring and fall. For rates and availability of beds, call 520-558-2396 or visit research.amnh.org/swrs/.

Hot Springs

The same processes that continue to shape the mountains and valleys of Southeastern Arizona contribute to the geothermal activity and presence of wells with naturally heated water. North of the Chiricahuas, the area around Safford at the base of the Pinaleño Mountains is known for its hot springs, each with its own personality. Those listed here are easy to reach.

Essence of Tranquility This spa is rustic, funky, friendly, and fun. The water from a hot well 167 feet deep is directed into one outdoor communal tub and six private tubs, decorated in varying themes. After your soak, you can have a massage or herbal wrap. Tub rental: $5/hour per person. Rental teepees sleep one to nine people. The office is open Tues.–Sat. 8 a.m.–6 p.m. at 6074 Lebanon Loop, Safford, AZ 85546. From U.S. Hwy. 191, turn west on Lebanon Road and follow the curve to the left. For reservations, call toll-free 877-895-6810 or visit www.geocities.com/essenceoftranquility.

Mexican star blossoms in the grasslands of Fort Huachuca. MILLS TANDY

BILLIONS OF STARS
IN THE BLACK NIGHT

THE LATE SCIENCE WRITER CARL SAGAN was famous for talking about the "billions and billions" of stars in the universe. When city-dwellers spend an evening in rural Southeastern Arizona, they feel as though they can see all those billions of stars twinkling above them. The clear air, dry climate, and relatively small population that produces artificial light are the reasons so many stars are visible. Astronomers from all over the world come to two major telescope complexes in Southeastern Arizona to take advantage of the dark, clear night skies.

Whipple Observatory

At the Fred Lawrence Whipple Observatory atop 8,500-foot Mount Hopkins in the Santa Rita Mountains, you have left the dust of the valley far below. The observatory is operated by the Smithsonian Institution Astrophysical Observatory in conjunction with several government agencies and universities from throughout the United States, England, and Ireland.

Optical telescopes and reflectors at Whipple Observatory, Mount Hopkins, in the Santa Rita Mountains. RANDY PRENTICE

To visit the Whipple Observatory, you must begin at the visitors center below. You'll learn the history of astronomy and how 21st-century instruments are helping the scientists who work here look ever more deeply into the universe.

If you've booked an all-day tour of the mountain, you'll be taken up a hair-raising 18-mile one-way road to the telescope complex. While most of the tour involves a discussion of serious science, visitors can indulge in some lighter moments next to the multiple-mirror gamma-ray collector, where their reflections have a fun-house quality.

Mount Graham International Observatory

Discovery Park in Safford is the gateway to Mount Graham International Observatory, home of the world's most powerful telescope. The staff at Discovery Park strives to make learning about the universe entertaining. A display details 14 different belief systems of how the universe was formed, including a video about the astronomers' conception of the birth of the universe, the Big Bang Theory. A flight simulator gives visitors a *Star Trek*-type ride through the solar system using NASA footage. On clear nights, a 20-inch telescope donated by the University of Arizona is open for sky viewing. Additional displays are nearing completion, and there is a lovely small pond with a comfortable blind for observing birds and other wildlife.

Those who take a tour of the International Observatory will be transported to the top of Mount Graham, where they'll see the Vatican Advanced Technology Telescope and the Heinrich Hertz Submillimeter Telescope, the world's most accurate radio telescope. The brand-new, large Binocular Telescope, the most powerful in the world, is a joint venture by the University of Arizona, Ohio State University, Research Corporation in Tucson, and Italian and German astronomical communities. Astronomers will use the telescope to search for extremely distant and faint objects such as ancient galaxies and quasars, to unravel the mysteries of how stars are born, and ultimately to search for life outside the solar system.

Try It Yourself If a trip to one of the major observatories has you wishing to spend time viewing the Orion Nebula or Jupiter and its moons for yourself, two smaller observatories near Benson can provide you with a personal eye-on-the-eyepiece night-sky viewing experience.

The Vega-Bray Observatory, just east of Benson, has eight major telescopes, a sliding-roof observatory room, and a planetarium. You can even watch the sun through safe, filtered telescopes. Beginners can choose a program that includes the guidance of an experienced astronomer; experienced stargazers can rent time to use the telescopes or bring their own equipment. The associated Sky Watcher's Inn B&B gives you a nearby bed to fall into when you've seen enough stars.

At the Deep Sky Ranch Observatory, owner Rich Dillon picks guests up at Benson-area lodgings and drives them down the dark dirt road to his observatory for Sky Wrangling classes. During an informal program, he finds the best views of the evening and shares them with his guests. His facilities include a 900-square-foot observatory with a retractable roof.

Fred Lawrence Whipple Observatory
The visitors center is open Mon.–Fri., 9 a.m.–4:30 p.m. Closed federal holidays. Tours of the observatory are conducted on Mon., Wed., and Fri., 9 a.m.–3 p.m., mid-March–Nov. Pack your own lunch for the noon picnic. Admission: adults $7, children 6–12 $2.50. No children under 6 permitted. Take exit 56 off I-19, and then drive along the eastside frontage road south three miles to Elephant Head Road. Drive east to Mount Hopkins Road. Turn right and go seven miles to the visitors center. For reservations and further information, call 520-670-5707 or visit cfa-www.harvard.edu/cfa/ep/flwo.html.

Mount Graham International Observatory
Discovery Park is open 6–10 p.m. Fri.–Sat. Admission: adults $4, children 6–11 $3, kids 5 and under free. Additional fees charged for rides. Tours to Mount Graham International Observatory operate Sat. 10 a.m.–5:30 p.m., May–Nov., weather permitting. Admission fee: $20 includes lunch. Not suitable for children under 8. Meet at the Chamber of Commerce, 1111 W. Thatcher Blvd. (U.S. Hwy. 70) in Safford. For reservations and further information, call 888-837-1841 or visit mgpc3.as.arizona.edu.

Deep Sky Ranch Observatory
For reservations, transportation, or further information, call 520-586-3730.

Vega-Bray Observatory and Sky Watcher's Inn
For information and reservations, call 520-615-3886 or visit www.communiverse.com/skywatcher.

Hot Well Dunes Recreation Area This remote hot spring is reached by a well-graded dirt road that parallels U.S. Hwy. 191 a few miles to the east. Off-road vehicle enthusiasts of all stripes are invited to cruise and roar over the large sand dunes in the area, so you will not find much tranquility on weekends. The 106-degree water is directed into two basins with a shallower pool between that is perfect for kids. The Bureau of Land Management collects a daily use fee of $3/person. Take U.S. Hwy. 70 about eight miles east of Safford, turn south on Haekel Road, bear to the left at the fork, and go 25 miles to the well-marked entrance. For further information, call 928-348-4400 or visit azwww.az.blm.gov/sfo/hot_well/hotwell.html.

Kachina Hot Springs Artesian Mineral Spa This is an elaborate business in a modern building that looks like it might be a warehouse. But inside are bright rooms, tile-lined tubs that are emptied and refilled after every use, and massage tables where you can relax and choose from an interesting menu of treatments. A soak in the hot mineral bath costs $7; add a sweat wrap for another $8. Open Memorial Day–Labor Day, Wed.–Sat. 9 a.m.–5 p.m.; Labor Day–Memorial Day, Mon.–Sat. 9 a.m.–5 p.m. 1155 W. Cactus Rd., Safford. From U.S. Hwy. 191, turn west on Cactus Road and follow the signs. For reservations, call 928-428-7212 or visit www.kachinasprings.com.

Roper Lake State Park This stone-lined, open-air hot spring is available to anyone using the park. Because it is quite small, you probably wouldn't want to share it with more than three other people unless they were close friends. Park entrance fee: $5/car. Camping: $10/day per vehicle. The tub is open daily until 10 p.m. 101 E. Roper Lake Rd., Safford, AZ 85546. Turn east from U.S. Hwy. 191 at the sign, about six miles south of Safford. For further information, call 928-428-6760 or go to www.pr.state.az.us/parkhtml/roper.html.

ANNUAL EVENTS

JANUARY
- SIERRA STAMPEDE, Sierra Vista. All women's pro rodeo.
- WINGS OVER WILLCOX, Willcox. Return of the wintering sandhill cranes, talks, workshops.

FEBRUARY
- COCHISE COUNTY COWBOY POETRY AND MUSIC GATHERING, Sierra Vista.
- INTERNATIONAL MARIACHI AND PIÑATA FESTIVAL, Douglas. Mariachi bands from Arizona and Sonora face off.
- MINIATURE ART SHOW, Willcox. National juried show.
- FESTIVAL OF THE ARTS, Tubac. Juried artists, entertainment.
- PIONEER WOMEN OF THE OLD WEST, Tombstone.
- TERRITORIAL DAYS, Benson.
- WESTERN HERITAGE WEEK, Sierra Vista.
- WESTERN SONGS at the Arizona Folklore Preserve, Ramsey Canyon.

MARCH
- COWBOY POETRY AND TALL TALE SESSION, Bisbee.
- TERRITORIAL DAYS, Tombstone.

APRIL
- GRAHAM COUNTY HORSE RACES, Safford.
- LA VUELTA DE BISBEE, a three-day bicycle race.
- MARIACHI FESTIVAL, Nogales. Regional mariachi bands.
- SOUTHEASTERN ARIZONA FINE ART SHOW, Willcox.
- TOMBSTONE ROSE FESTIVAL. Celebrating Tombstone pioneers and the world's largest rosebush.

MAY
- ANTIQUE SHOW, Bisbee.
- CINCO DE MAYO CELEBRATION, Douglas. In honor of Mexico's victory over France in 1862.
- COTTON 'N' COPPER STAMPEDE RODEO, Safford.
- FIESTA DE LA PRIMAVERA, Holy Trinity Monastery, St. David.
- SALUTE TO THE BUFFALO SOLDIER, Sierra Vista. Commemorating African-American troops.
- SPRING ARTS FESTIVAL, Bisbee. Plein-air paint-athon and gallery walk.
- WYATT EARP DAYS, Tombstone.

These Czechoslovakian rock climbers visited the Whetstone Mountains to practice their skills on a site known to adventurers as "Celebrity Cave." ANDREW KORNYLAK

JUNE
- DOG DAYS OF SUMMER, Fort Huachuca. Outdoor concerts.
- FESTIVAL OF COLOR HOT-AIR BALLOON RALLY, Willcox.
- RAILROAD DAYS, Benson.
- SONOITA QUARTER HORSE SHOW, Sonoita. Oldest quarter horse show in the country.

JULY
- FOURTH OF JULY festivities in many towns.
- GRAHAM COUNTY PIONEER DAYS, rotates among Safford, Thatcher, and Pima.

AUGUST
- ARIZONA JUNIOR RODEO, Douglas.
- POETRY FESTIVAL, Bisbee.
- SOUTHWEST WINGS BIRDING FESTIVAL, Sierra Vista. Field trips, lectures, and owl prowls.
- PEACH FESTIVAL, Willcox.
- VIGILANTE DAYS, Tombstone.

SEPTEMBER
- BREWERY GULCH DAYS, Bisbee.
- CIDER FESTIVAL, Willcox.
- COCHISE COUNTY FAIR, Douglas.
- COCHISE DAYS FESTIVAL, Pearce/Sunsites.
- COWBOY POETRY AND MUSIC FESTIVAL, Safford.
- GILA VALLEY COWBOY POETRY AND MUSIC ROUNDUP, Safford.
- MEXICAN INDEPENDENCE DAY, Douglas. Celebrate in this Arizona/Sonora border town.
- OKTOBERFEST, Sierra Vista. Town's annual German celebration.
- RENDEZVOUS OF GUNFIGHTERS, Tombstone. Gunfighter groups in national competition.

OCTOBER

- ANZA DAYS, Presidio State Park, Tubac. Honors Juan Bautista de Anza, Tubac captain.
- ART IN THE PARK, Sierra Vista.
- BISBEE STAIR CLIMB RACE. 1,034 stairs included in a 5K race.
- GEM AND MINERAL SHOW, Bisbee.
- GRAHAM COUNTY FAIR, Safford.
- FALL FESTIVAL AND GYMKHANA, Elfrida.
- HAUNTED MINE TOUR, Bisbee.
- HELLDORADO DAYS, Tombstone.
- HOT-AIR BALLOON FESTIVAL, Sierra Vista.
- PATAGONIA FALL FESTIVAL, Patagonia.
- REX ALLEN DAYS and COWBOY HALL OF FAME INDUCTION, Willcox.

NOVEMBER

- ARTS FESTIVAL, Holy Trinity Monastery, St. David.
- COWBOY CHRISTMAS ARTS AND CRAFTS SHOW, Safford.
- FIBER ARTS FESTIVAL, Bisbee. Weaving, spinning, and exhibits.
- HISTORIC HOME TOUR and FESTIVAL OF LIGHTS, Bisbee.
- EMMETT KELLY JR. DAYS, Tombstone. Includes national Clown Roundup.
- CLANTON GANG REUNION, Tombstone. Speakers and look-alike contests.
- NATIVE AMERICAN POWWOW, Sierra Vista.
- ST. MARTIN'S NEW RELEASE FESTIVAL, Sonoita Vineyards Winery, Elgin.

DECEMBER

- ANNUAL AUDUBON CHRISTMAS BIRD COUNT, Sierra Vista and Portal.
- CASCABEL CHRISTMAS FAIR, Cascabel.
- CHRISTMAS APPLE FESTIVAL, Willcox.
- CHRISTMAS LIGHT PARADE, Douglas.
- FIESTA DE LA NAVIDAD, Tubac. Luminarias and carolers.
- HISTORIC HOME TOUR, Tombstone.
- HISTORIC OFFICERS' HOME TOUR, Fort Huachuca/ Sierra Vista.
- LA FIESTA DE TUMACÁCORI, Tumacácori. Food, music, and tours at the historic mission.
- LAS POSADAS, Nogales. Traditional Mexican event commemorating Mary and Joseph's search for lodging.

RESOURCES

BENSON/SAN PEDRO VALLEY VISITOR CENTER
249 E. 4th St., Benson, AZ 85602, 520-586-4293

GREATER BISBEE CHAMBER OF COMMERCE AND VISITOR CENTER P.O. Box BA, Bisbee, AZ 85603, 520-432-5421 or 520-866-BISBEE, www.bisbeearizona.com

BUREAU OF LAND MANAGEMENT Arizona State Office, 222 N. Central Ave., Phoenix, AZ 85004, 602-417-9200, azwww.az.blm.gov/azso.htm

DOUGLAS CHAMBER OF COMMERCE
341 10th St., Douglas, AZ 85607, 520-364-2477, www.discoverdouglas.com

THE NATURE CONSERVANCY 1510 Fort Lowell Rd., Tucson, AZ 85719, 520-622-3861, www.tncarizona.org

NOGALES/SANTA CRUZ COUNTY CHAMBER OF COMMERCE Kino Park, Nogales, AZ 85621, 520-287-3685, www.nogaleschamber.com

PATAGONIA VISITOR INFORMATION
307 McKeown Ave., P.O. Box 241, Patagonia, AZ 85624, 888-794-0060, www.patagoniaaz.com

PEARCE-SUNSITES TOURIST CENTER 133A Frontage Rd., P.O. Box 308, Pearce, AZ 85625, 520-826-3535

SIERRA VISTA CONVENTION AND VISITORS BUREAU 21 E. Willcox Dr., Sierra Vista, AZ 85635, 800-288-3861, www.visitsierravista.com

SONOITA-ELGIN CHAMBER OF COMMERCE
P.O. Box 607, Sonoita, AZ 85637, 520-455-5498, www.nogaleschamber.com/travel/sonoita.html

SULPHUR SPRINGS VALLEY CHAMBER OF COMMERCE P.O. Box 614, Elfrida, AZ 85610, 520-642-1200, www.elfridachamber.org

TOMBSTONE CHAMBER OF COMMERCE
P.O. Box 995, Tombstone, AZ 85638, 888-457-3929, www.tombstone.org

TUBAC CHAMBER OF COMMERCE P.O. Box 1866, Tubac, AZ 85646, 520-398-2704, www.tubacaz.com

WILLCOX CHAMBER OF COMMERCE 1500 North Circle I Rd., Willcox, AZ 85643, 800-200-2272, www.willcoxchamber.com

BOOKS: Good Traveling Companions

Whether you're planning a trip, in the middle of a journey, or reminiscing about the wonderful time you had, it's fun to read books about the areas of your visit. The books below focus on the people, places, events, flora, and fauna of Southeastern Arizona or contain information of particular significance to the area.

Biographies, diaries & memoirs

Aleshire, Peter. *Cochise: The Life and Times of the Great Apache Chief*. New York: John Wiley & Sons, 2001.

——. *The Fox and the Whirlwind: General George Crook and Geronimo, a Paired Biography*. New York: John Wiley & Sons, 2000.

Bell, Bob Boze. *The Illustrated Life and Times of Doc Holliday*, second ed. Tri-Star–Boze Publications, Inc., 1995.

———. *The Illustrated Life and Times of Wyatt Earp*, fourth ed. Tri-Star–Boze Publications, Inc., 1994.

Burns, Roger A. *Desert Honkytonk: The Story of Tombstone's Bird Cage Theatre*. Golden, Colo.: Fulcrum Publishing, 2000.

Geronimo and S.M. Barrett. *Geronimo: His Own Story*, rev. ed. New York: Penguin Group, 1996.

Hickey, Michael M. *Street Fight in Tombstone, Near the O.K. Corral*. Honolulu, Hawaii: Talei Publishers, 1991.

Sharp, Robert L. *Bob Sharp's Cattle Country: Rawhide Ranching on Both Sides of the Border*. Tucson, Ariz.: University of Arizona Press, 1985.

Shelton, Richard. *Going Back to Bisbee*. Tucson, Ariz.: University of Arizona Press, 1992.

Summerhayes, Martha. *Vanished Arizona: Recollections of the Army Life of a New England Woman*. Lincoln, Neb.: University of Nebraska Press, 1979.

Tefertiller, Casey. *Wyatt Earp: The Life behind the Legend*. New York: John Wiley & Sons, 1992.

Bird-watching

Kaufman, Lynn Hassler. *Birds of the American Southwest*. Tucson, Ariz.: Rio Nuevo Publishers, 2000.

——. *Hummingbirds of the American West*. Tucson, Ariz.: Rio Nuevo Publishers, 2001.

Tweit, Joan, ed. *Finding Birds in Southeastern Arizona*. Tucson, Ariz.: Audubon Society, 1999.

Vezo, Tom, and Richard L. Glinski. *Birds of Prey in the American West*. Tucson, Ariz.: Rio Nuevo Publishers, 2002.

Fiction

Arnold, Elliot. *Blood Brother*. Lincoln, Neb.: Bison Books, 1979.

Hartmann, William K. *Cities of Gold*. New York: Forge Books, 2002.

Houston, Robert. *Bisbee 17: A Novel*. Tucson, Ariz.: University of Arizona Press, 1999.

Jance, J.A. *Outlaw Mountain*. New York: Avon, 2000.

——. *Paradise Lost*. New York: Avon, 2002.

——. *Rattlesnake Crossing*. New York: Avon, 1999.

——. *Skeleton Canyon*. New York: Avon, 1998.

Noble, Marguerite. *Filaree: A Novel of an American Woman*. Albuquerque, N.M.: University of New Mexico Press, 1985.

Thornton, Betsy. *Ghost Towns*. New York: St. Martin's Press, 2003.

——. *High Lonesome Road*. New York: St. Martin's Press, 2001

Williams, Jeanne. *Woman of Three Worlds*. iUniverse.com, 2000.

History

Griffith, Jim. *Saints of the Southwest*. Tucson, Ariz.: Rio Nuevo Publishers, 2000.

Hayes, Alden. *Portal to Paradise: 11,537 Years, More or Less, on the Northeast Slope of the Chiricahua Mountains*. Tucson, Ariz.: University of Arizona Press, 1999.

Myers, John Myers. *Tombstone's Early Years*. Lincoln, Neb.: University of Nebraska Press, 1995.

Sheridan, Thomas E. *Arizona: A History*. Tucson, Ariz.: University of Arizona Press, 1995.

Stockel, H. Henrietta. *Chiricahua Apache Women and Children: Safekeepers of the Heritage*. College Station, Tex.: Texas A&M Press, 2000.

Trimble, Marshall. *Arizona: A Cavalcade of History*, rev ed. Tucson, Ariz.: Rio Nuevo Publishers, 2003.

Natural history

Broyles, William. *Our Sonoran Desert.* Tucson, Ariz.: Rio Nuevo Publishers, 2003.

Lowry, Joe Dan, and Joe P. Lowry. *Turquoise Unearthed: An Illustrated Guide.* Tucson, Ariz.: Rio Nuevo Publishers, 2002.

Niethammer, Carolyn. *American Indian Cooking: Recipes from the Southwest,* second ed. Lincoln, Neb.: University of Nebraska Press, 2001.

Phillips, Steven J. (ed.) et al. *A Natural History of the Sonoran Desert.* Tucson, Ariz. and Berkeley, Calif.: Arizona-Sonora Desert Museum and University of California Press, 1999.

Quinn, Meg. *Cacti of the Desert Southwest.* Tucson, Ariz.: Rio Nuevo Publishers, 2001.

——. *Wildflowers of the Desert Southwest.* Tucson, Ariz.: Rio Nuevo Publishers, 2000.

——. *Wildflowers of the Mountain Southwest.* Tucson, Ariz.: Rio Nuevo Publishers, 2003.

Taylor, Leonard. *Discover the San Pedro Valley: Your Complete Field Guide to a Valley Rich in Scenery, History, and Natural Recreation Opportunities.* Bisbee, Ariz.: Agave Guides, 2000.

Taylor, Richard Cachor. *Trogons of the Arizona Borderlands.* Tucson, Ariz.: Treasure Chest Publications, 1994.

Williamson, Sheri L. *A Field Guide to Hummingbirds of North America.* New York: Houghton Mifflin, 2001.

CREDITS

Front cover: sacred datura plant in the Dragoon Mountains, by Tom Danielsen; top inset: Sam and Mac Donaldson, by W. Ross Humphreys; lower inset: painted lady butterfly, Mount Graham, by Bernadette Heath

Back cover, clockwise from top left: Tumacácori National Monument, by Randy Prentice; John Slaughter Ranch, by Bernadette Heath; woodcut by Sam Donaldson; Natchez and Geronimo, by A. F. Randall (photo courtesy of Robert McCubbin)

Across from title page: autumn in Miller Canyon, by Randy Prentice

Table of contents: Willcox Playa, by Jack Dykinga; inset: Tombstone Courthouse State Historic Park, by Laurence Parent

Other photographs: Historic photographs facing page one and on pages 6, 31, 38–39 (bottom), 50–51 (bottom), 51 (top), and 56–57 courtesy of the Bisbee Mining & Historical Museum. B-Troop photo on page 5 courtesy of the Sierra Vista Convention & Visitors Bureau. *Red River* photo on page 12 courtesy of the Santa Cruz Cowbelles Western Heritage Center. Tubac Golf Resort photo on page 23 courtesy of Tubac Golf Resort. Natchez and Geronimo photo on page 55 by A. F. Randall, courtesy of Robert McCubbin.

Photography and illustration © as follows:

Walt Anderson: page 27

Alysa Bennett: pages 2, 4, 7 (bottom), 41, 43

Tom Danielsen: front cover

Sam Donaldson: back cover (lower right), 29 (top), 61 (top), 63 (top) Jay Dusard: pages 60, 62 (bottom)

Jack Dykinga: table of contents, pages 30, 44

Bernadette Heath: front cover (lower inset), back cover (top right), pages 8, 24, 38 (top), 61 (bottom), 62 (top), 65 (bottom)

George H. H. Huey: pages 14, 52, 53

W. Ross Humphreys: front cover (top inset), page 22

Gill C. Kenny: page 20

Andrew Kornylak: pages 1, 34-35, 70

Larry Lindahl: pages 3 (bottom), 10, 28, 37, 49

C. Allan Morgan: page 46

Carolyn Neithammer: page 16

Laurence Parent: table of contents inset, pages 32–33, 64

Randy Prentice: back cover (top left), facing title page, pages 13, 15, 17, 18, 19, 36, 40, 65 (top), 68

J. Keith Schreiber: pages 11, 48

Scott T. Smith: page 54

Mills Tandy: pages 7 (top), 29 (bottom), 67

Larry Ulrich: pages 3 (top), 9

Tom Vezo: pages 21 (all), 23 (top), 25, 26, 45, 58–59, 66

Map on page 74 by Andy Mosier, © Madden Publishing and used with permission.

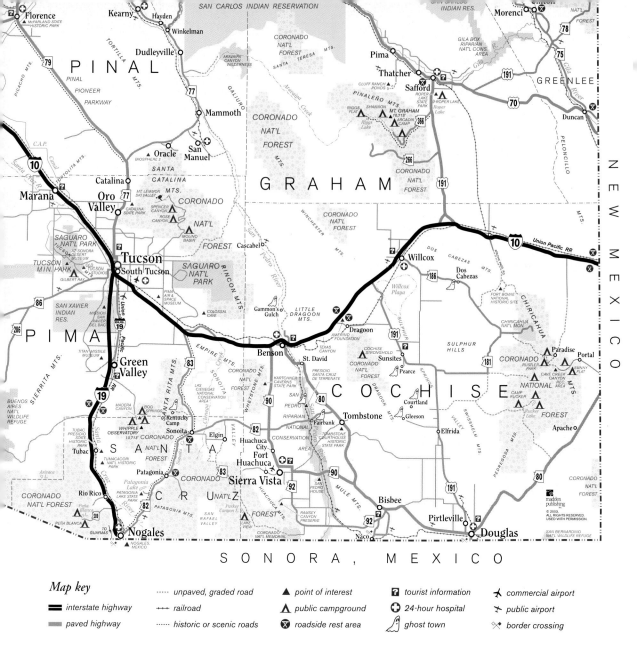

Map key

- ┅┅┅ unpaved, graded road
- ━━━ interstate highway
- ▬▬▬ paved highway
- ┼┼┼ railroad
- ┉┉┉ historic or scenic roads
- ▲ point of interest
- △ public campground
- ✕ roadside rest area
- 🅿 tourist information
- ✛ 24-hour hospital
- 👻 ghost town
- ✈ commercial airport
- ✈ public airport
- ✕✈ border crossing

About the Author

Carolyn Niethammer grew up outside Prescott, a small town in northern Arizona. After receiving a degree in journalism from the University of Arizona in Tucson, Carolyn worked for newspapers, then joined a group of friends hoping to start a new community in the then-abandoned town of Paradise on the eastern slopes of the Chiricahua Mountains. The dream was never realized and, after a season living in northern California, where she learned to gather wild greens and berries, she returned to Southern Arizona and began research on the edible wild foods of the Southwestern deserts. That interest led to two books, *American Indian Cooking: Recipes from the Southwest* and *Tumbleweed Gourmet*. She also wrote *Daughters of the Earth: The Lives and Legends of American Indian Women* and the award-winning *I'll Go and Do More: Annie Dodge Wauneka, Navajo Leader and Activist*. Her next project is a book about cooking with prickly pear cactus. Visit her online at www.cniethammer.com.